D0478441

THOR & LOKI
IN THE LAND OF GIANTS

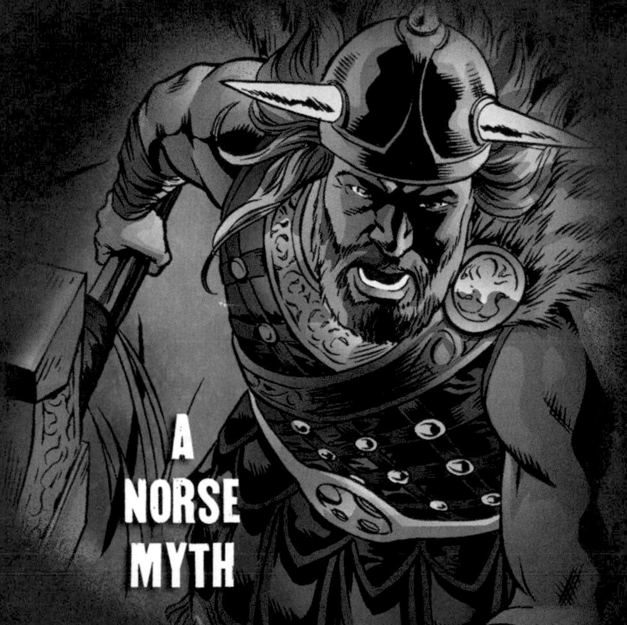

A NORSE MYTH

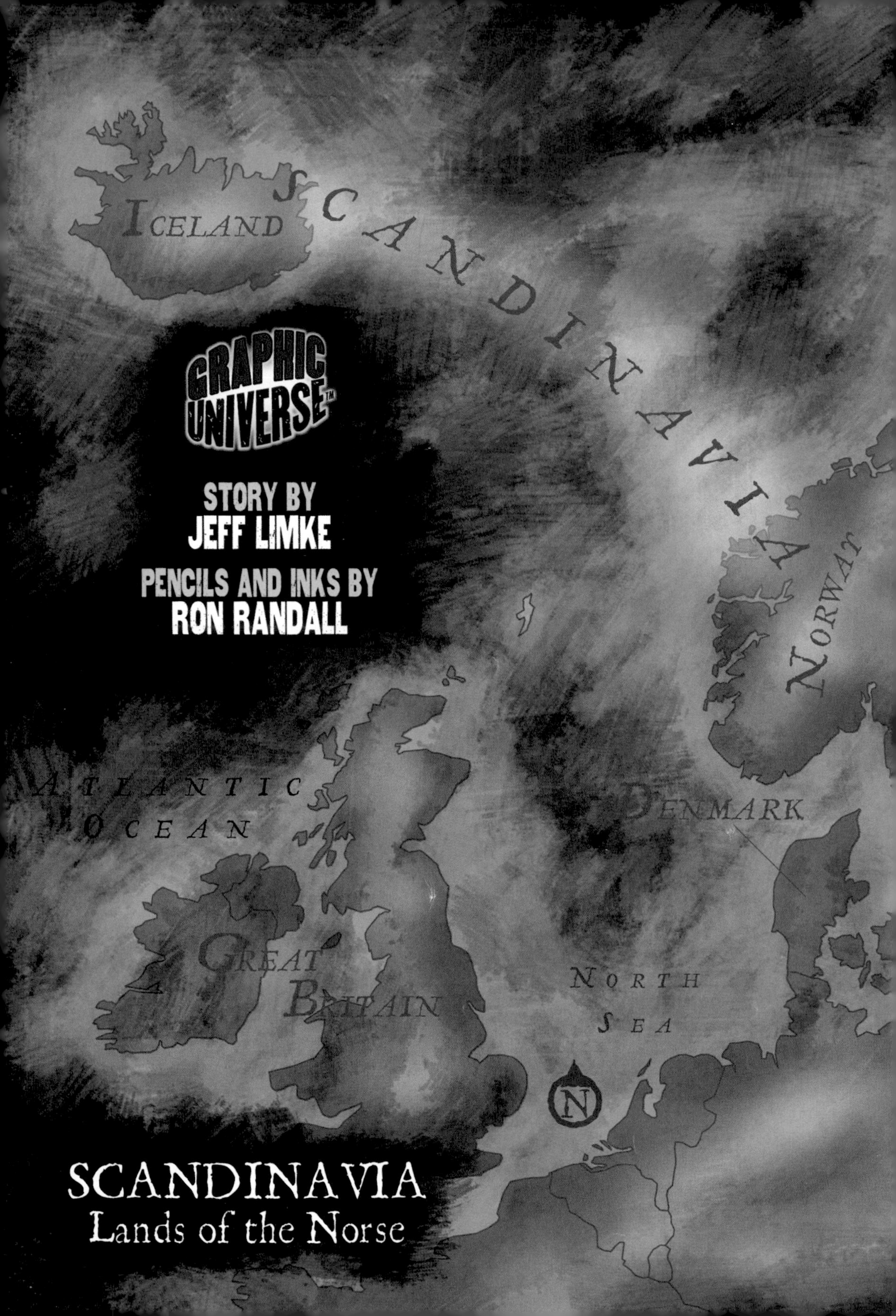
ICELAND
SCANDINAVIA
NORWAY
ATLANTIC OCEAN
DENMARK
GREAT BRITAIN
NORTH SEA
N

GRAPHIC UNIVERSE™

STORY BY
JEFF LIMKE
PENCILS AND INKS BY
RON RANDALL

SCANDINAVIA
Lands of the Norse

THOR & LOKI
IN THE LAND OF GIANTS

A NORSE MYTH

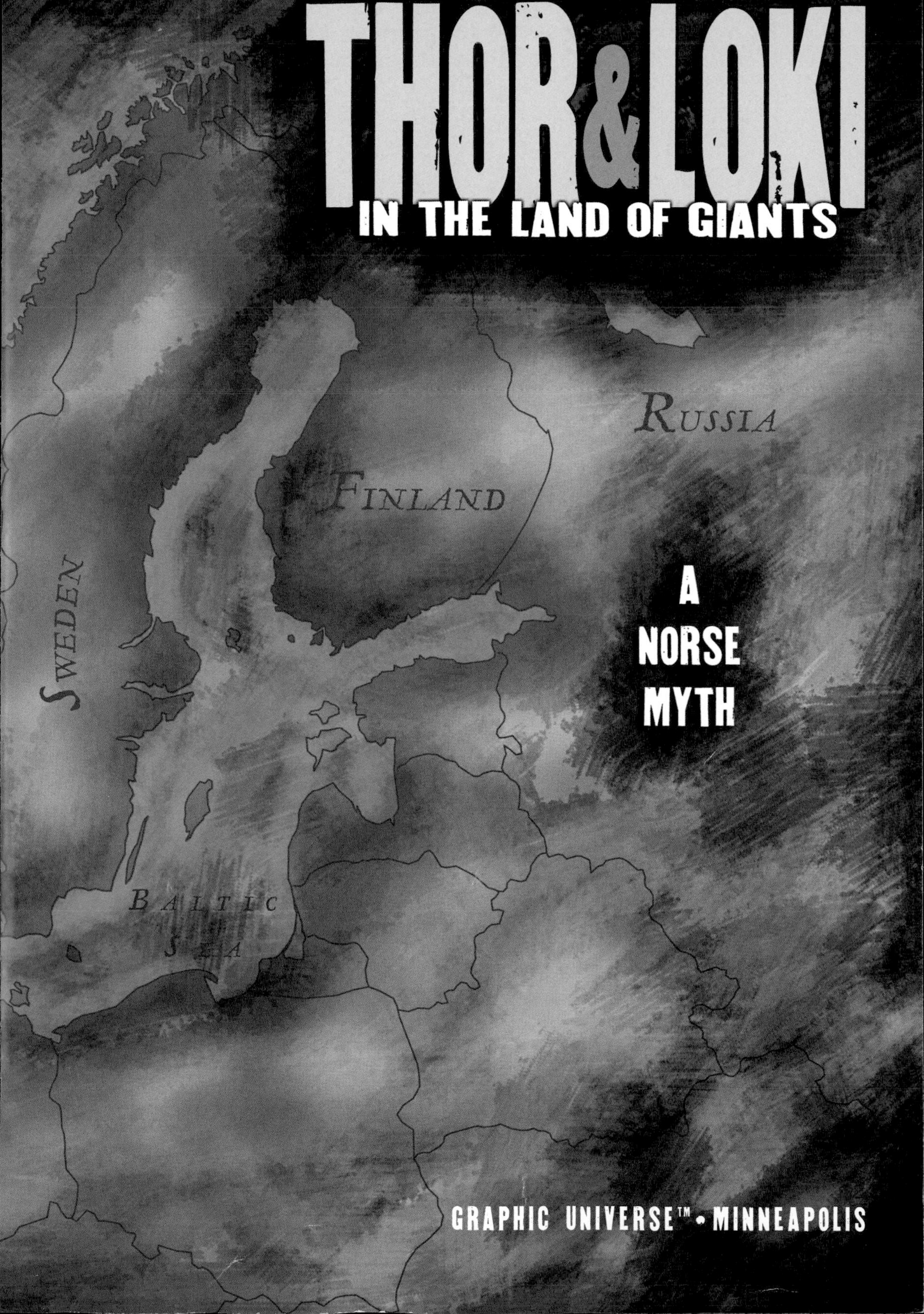
RUSSIA
FINLAND
SWEDEN
BALTIC SEA

GRAPHIC UNIVERSE™ • MINNEAPOLIS

Thor and Loki are two of the most famous of the legendary gods of Norse mythology. The stories of their adventures have been passed down through the medieval work the *Prose Edda*. This work was written around 1200 by Snorri Sturluson, a poet and politician living in Iceland. For this book, author Jeff Limke consulted modern retellings of Thor and Loki's legendary journey to the land of the Giants, including *Bulfinch's Mythology*, the classic work of American Thomas Bulfinch. Artist Ron Randall consulted numerous reference books on medieval Vikings as well as art from the ancient Norse period to bring to life the vivid images of this story.

STORY BY JEFF LIMKE

PENCILS AND INKS BY RON RANDALL

COLORING BY HI-FI DESIGN

LETTERING BY BILL HAUSER

Copyright © 2007 by Millbrook Press, Inc.

Graphic Universe™ is a trademark of Millbrook Press, Inc.

Graphic Universe™
An imprint of Lerner Publishing Group
241 First Avenue North
Minneapolis, MN 55401 U.S.A.

Website address: www.lernerbooks.com

Library of Congress Cataloging-in-Publication Data

Limke, Jeff.
    Thor and Loki : in the land of giants : a Norse myth / by Jeff Limke ; illustrated by Ron Randall.
       p.   cm. — (Graphic Myths and Legends)
    Includes bibliographical references.
    ISBN-13: 978-0-8225-3087-9 (lib. bdg. : alk. paper)
    ISBN-10: 0-8225-3087-2 (lib. bdg. : alk. paper)
    1. Thor (Norse deity)—Juvenile literature. 2. Loki (Norse deity)—Juvenile literature. I. Randall, Ron. II. Title. III. Series: Graphic myths and legends (Minneapolis, Minn.)
    BL870.T5L56 2007
    398.209363—dc22   2005033069

Manufactured in the United States of America
1 2 3 4 5 6 - JR - 12 11 10 09 08 07

TABLE OF CONTENTS

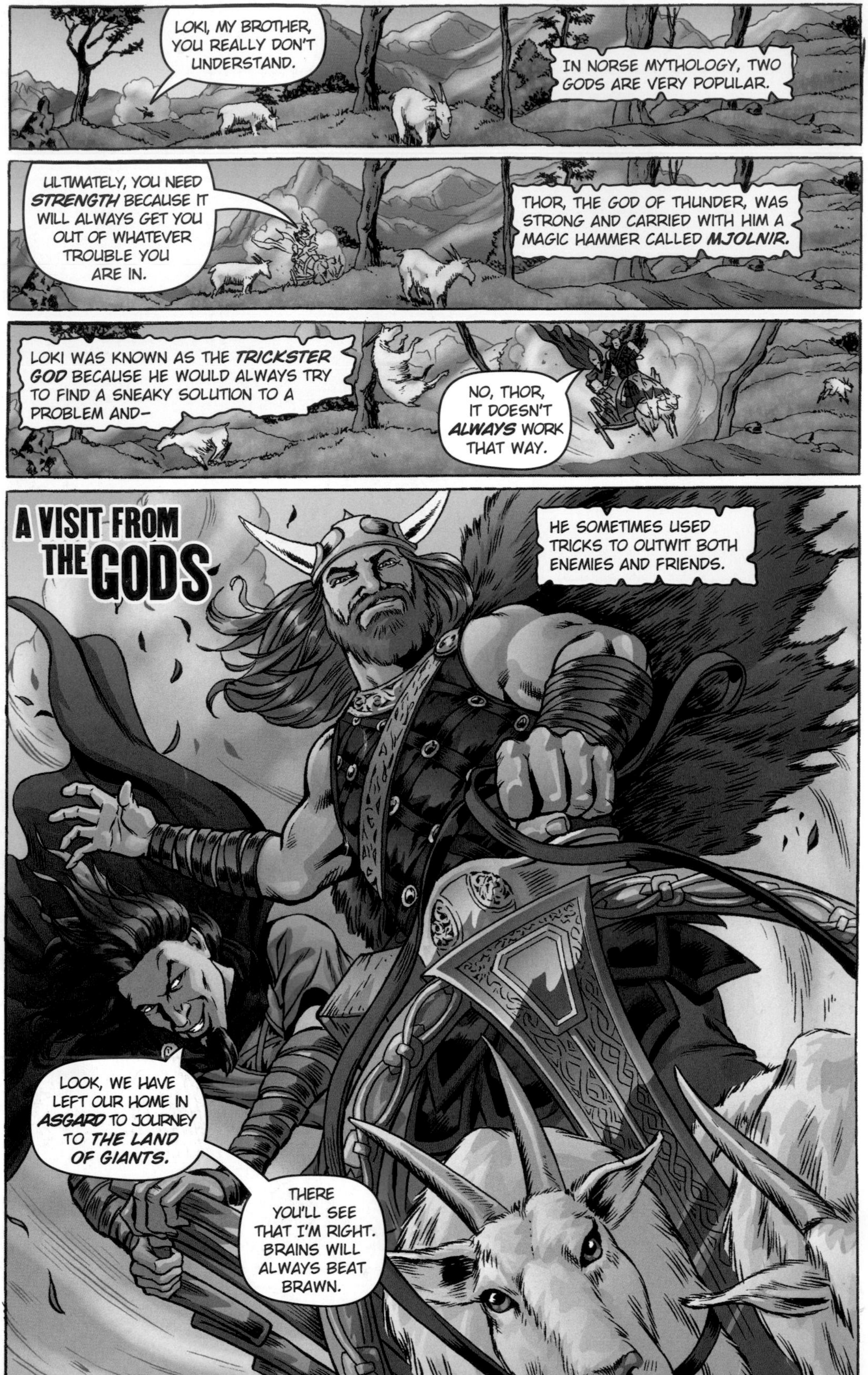
LOKI, MY BROTHER, YOU REALLY DON'T UNDERSTAND.
IN NORSE MYTHOLOGY, TWO GODS ARE VERY POPULAR.
ULTIMATELY, YOU NEED STRENGTH BECAUSE IT WILL ALWAYS GET YOU OUT OF WHATEVER TROUBLE YOU ARE IN.
THOR, THE GOD OF THUNDER, WAS STRONG AND CARRIED WITH HIM A MAGIC HAMMER CALLED MJOLNIR.
LOKI WAS KNOWN AS THE TRICKSTER GOD BECAUSE HE WOULD ALWAYS TRY TO FIND A SNEAKY SOLUTION TO A PROBLEM AND–
NO, THOR, IT DOESN'T ALWAYS WORK THAT WAY.
A VISIT FROM THE GODS
HE SOMETIMES USED TRICKS TO OUTWIT BOTH ENEMIES AND FRIENDS.
LOOK, WE HAVE LEFT OUR HOME IN ASGARD TO JOURNEY TO THE LAND OF GIANTS.
THERE YOU'LL SEE THAT I'M RIGHT. BRAINS WILL ALWAYS BEAT BRAWN.

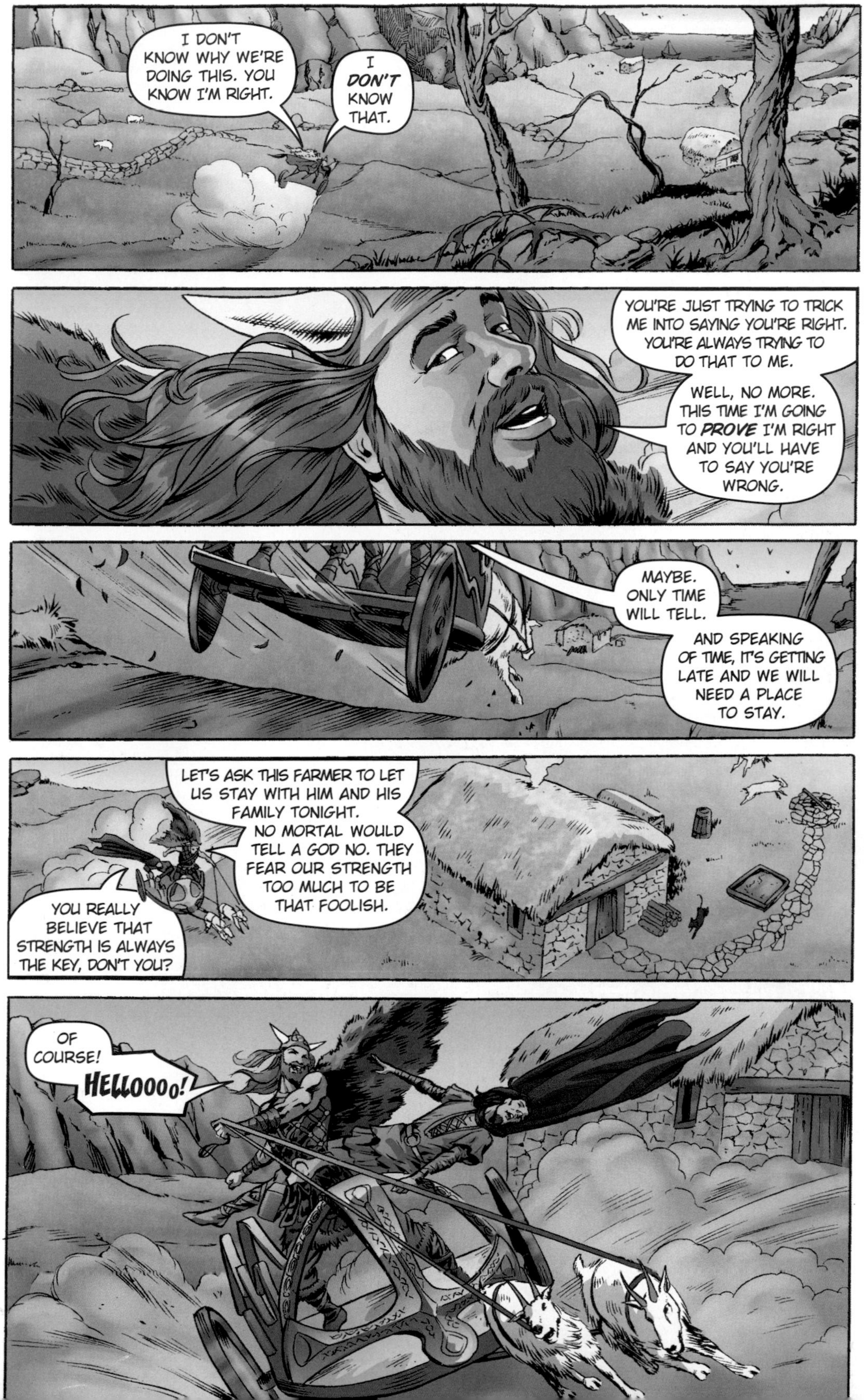
I DON'T KNOW WHY WE'RE DOING THIS. YOU KNOW I'M RIGHT.
I ***DON'T*** KNOW THAT.
YOU'RE JUST TRYING TO TRICK ME INTO SAYING YOU'RE RIGHT. YOU'RE ALWAYS TRYING TO DO THAT TO ME.
WELL, NO MORE. THIS TIME I'M GOING TO ***PROVE*** I'M RIGHT AND YOU'LL HAVE TO SAY YOU'RE WRONG.
MAYBE. ONLY TIME WILL TELL.
AND SPEAKING OF TIME, IT'S GETTING LATE AND WE WILL NEED A PLACE TO STAY.
LET'S ASK THIS FARMER TO LET US STAY WITH HIM AND HIS FAMILY TONIGHT.
NO MORTAL WOULD TELL A GOD NO. THEY FEAR OUR STRENGTH TOO MUCH TO BE THAT FOOLISH.
YOU REALLY BELIEVE THAT STRENGTH IS ALWAYS THE KEY, DON'T YOU?
OF COURSE!
HELLOOOO!

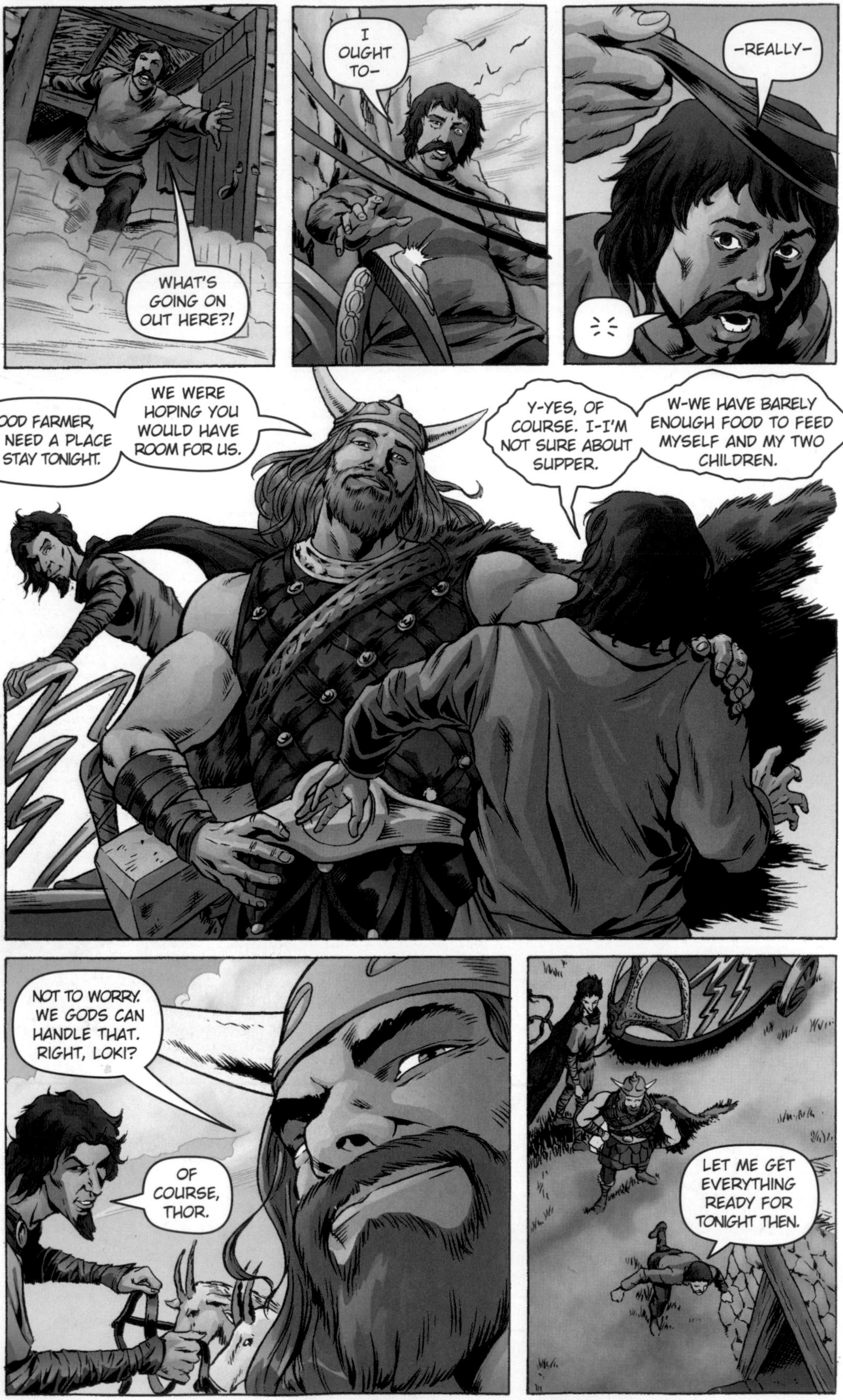
WHAT'S GOING ON OUT HERE?!
I OUGHT TO—
—REALLY—
GOOD FARMER, WE NEED A PLACE TO STAY TONIGHT.
WE WERE HOPING YOU WOULD HAVE ROOM FOR US.
Y-YES, OF COURSE. I-I'M NOT SURE ABOUT SUPPER.
W-WE HAVE BARELY ENOUGH FOOD TO FEED MYSELF AND MY TWO CHILDREN.
NOT TO WORRY. WE GODS CAN HANDLE THAT. RIGHT, LOKI?
OF COURSE, THOR.
LET ME GET EVERYTHING READY FOR TONIGHT THEN.

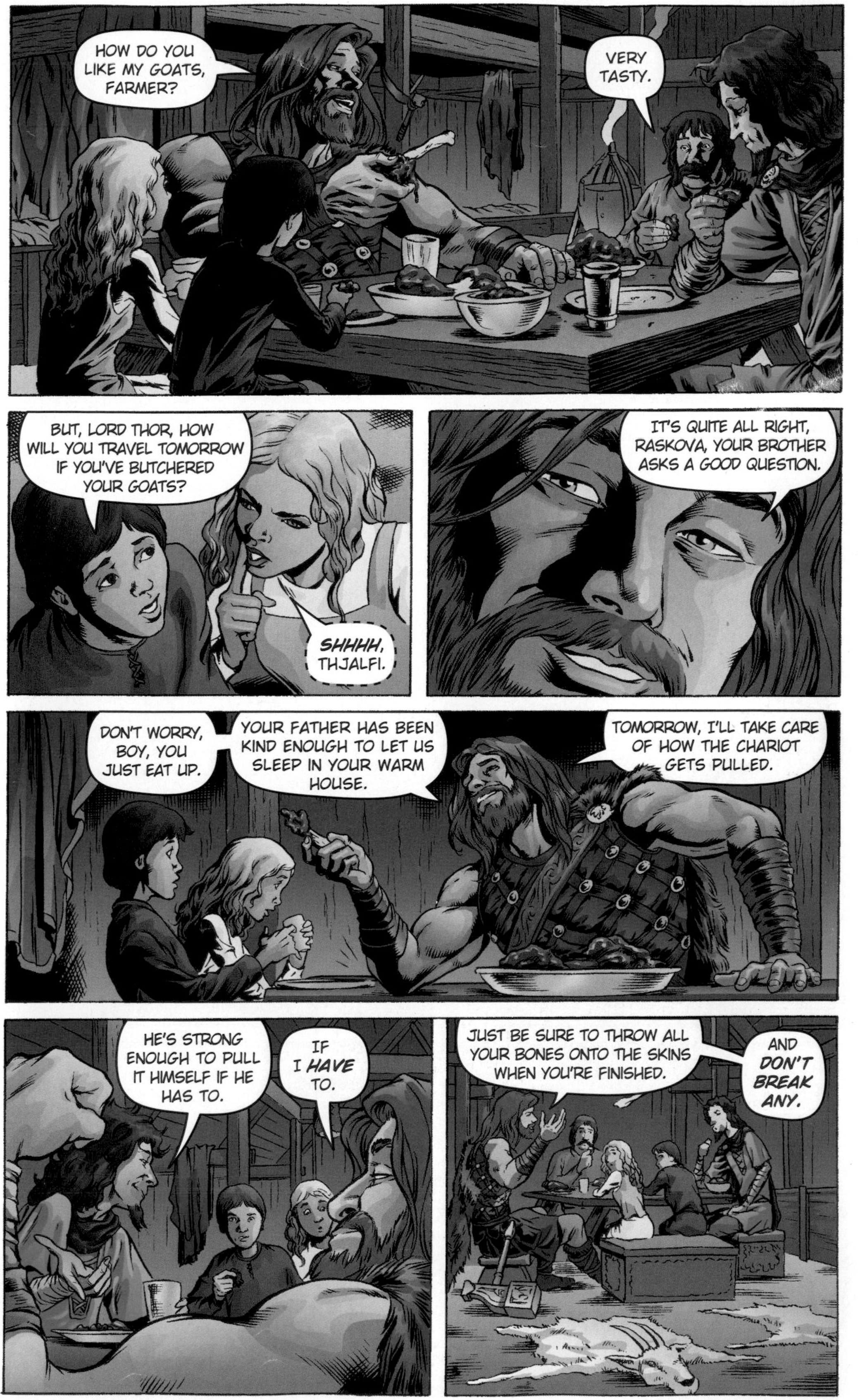
HOW DO YOU LIKE MY GOATS, FARMER?
VERY TASTY.
BUT, LORD THOR, HOW WILL YOU TRAVEL TOMORROW IF YOU'VE BUTCHERED YOUR GOATS?
SHHHH, THJALFI.
IT'S QUITE ALL RIGHT, RASKOVA, YOUR BROTHER ASKS A GOOD QUESTION.
DON'T WORRY, BOY, YOU JUST EAT UP.
YOUR FATHER HAS BEEN KIND ENOUGH TO LET US SLEEP IN YOUR WARM HOUSE.
TOMORROW, I'LL TAKE CARE OF HOW THE CHARIOT GETS PULLED.
HE'S STRONG ENOUGH TO PULL IT HIMSELF IF HE HAS TO.
IF I HAVE TO.
JUST BE SURE TO THROW ALL YOUR BONES ONTO THE SKINS WHEN YOU'RE FINISHED.
AND DON'T BREAK ANY.

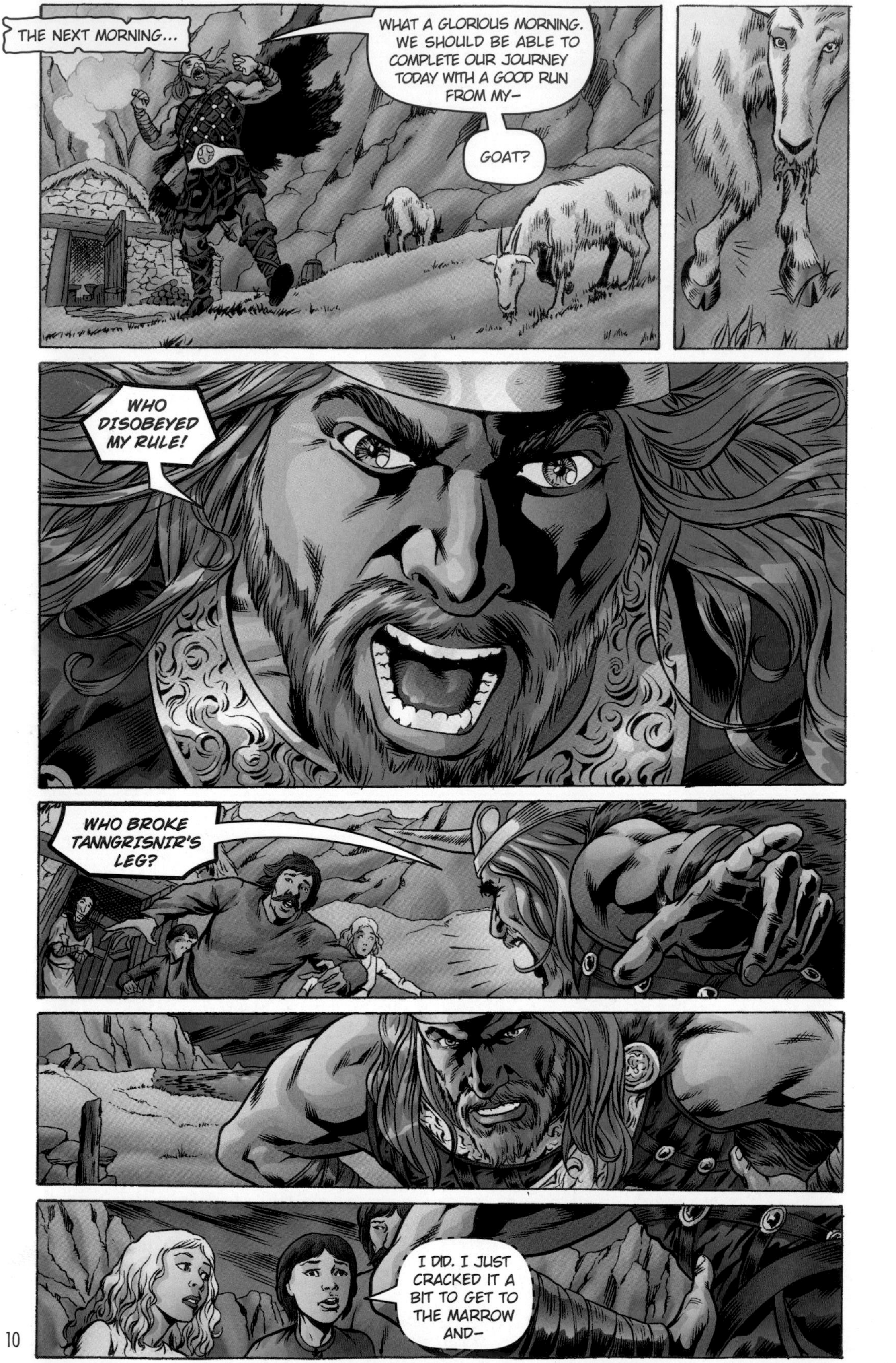
THE NEXT MORNING...
WHAT A GLORIOUS MORNING. WE SHOULD BE ABLE TO COMPLETE OUR JOURNEY TODAY WITH A GOOD RUN FROM MY-
GOAT?
WHO DISOBEYED MY RULE!
WHO BROKE TANNGRISNIR'S LEG?
I DID. I JUST CRACKED IT A BIT TO GET TO THE MARROW AND-

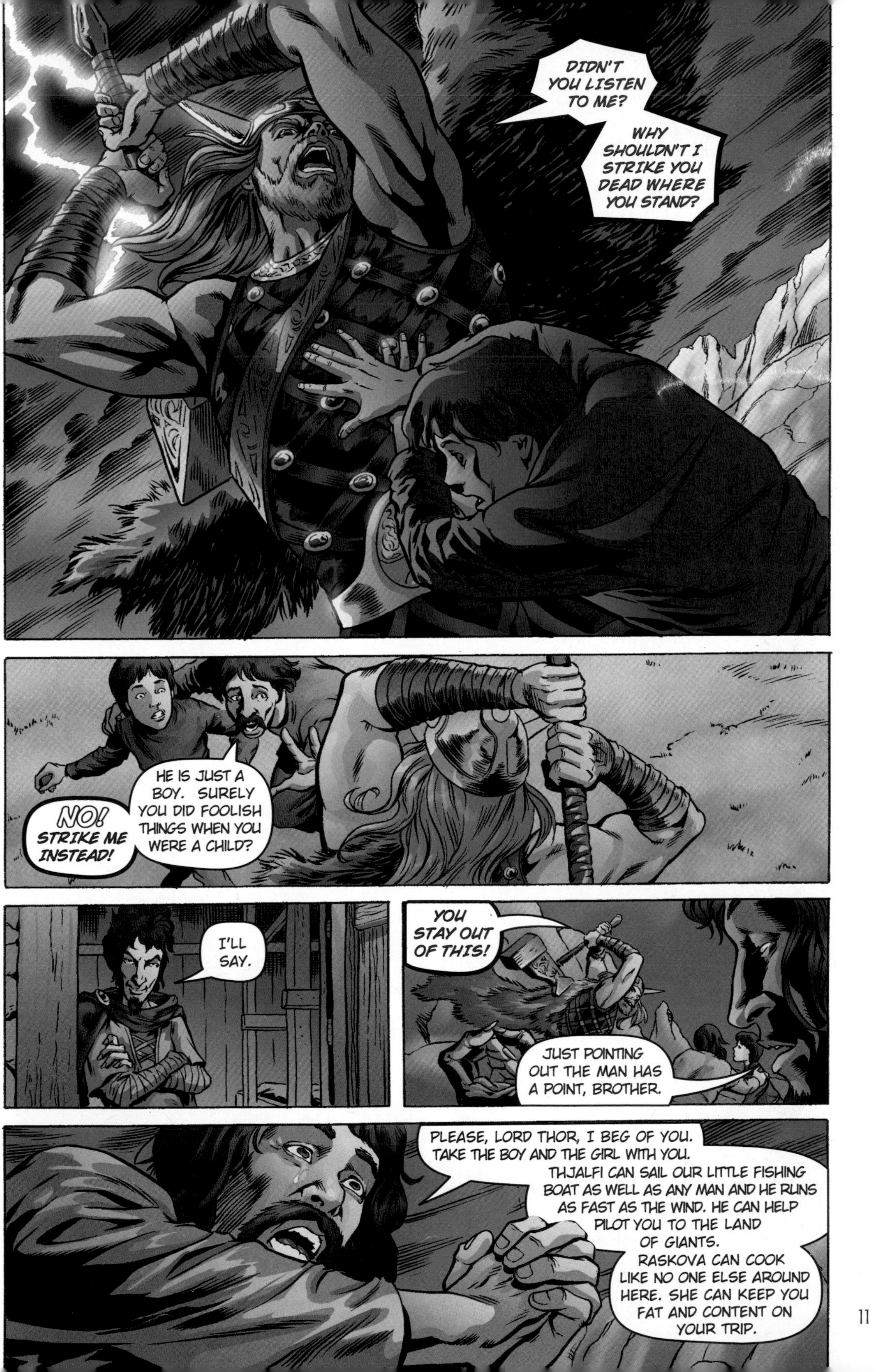

DIDN'T YOU LISTEN TO ME?
WHY SHOULDN'T I STRIKE YOU DEAD WHERE YOU STAND?
NO! STRIKE ME INSTEAD!
HE IS JUST A BOY. SURELY YOU DID FOOLISH THINGS WHEN YOU WERE A CHILD?
I'LL SAY.
YOU STAY OUT OF THIS!
JUST POINTING OUT THE MAN HAS A POINT, BROTHER.
PLEASE, LORD THOR, I BEG OF YOU. TAKE THE BOY AND THE GIRL WITH YOU.
THJALFI CAN SAIL OUR LITTLE FISHING BOAT AS WELL AS ANY MAN AND HE RUNS AS FAST AS THE WIND. HE CAN HELP PILOT YOU TO THE LAND OF GIANTS.
RASKOVA CAN COOK LIKE NO ONE ELSE AROUND HERE. SHE CAN KEEP YOU FAT AND CONTENT ON YOUR TRIP.

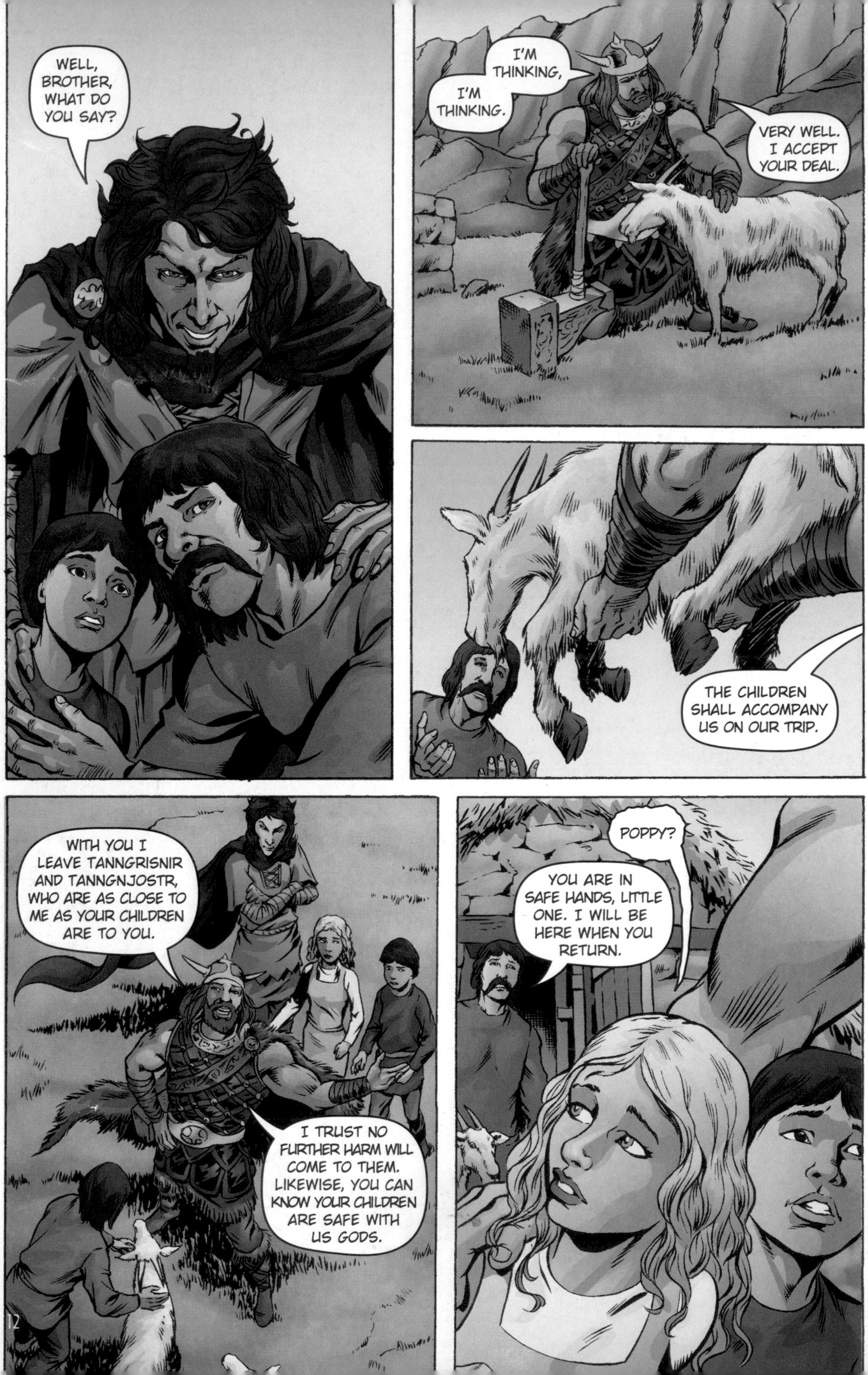
WELL, BROTHER, WHAT DO YOU SAY?
I'M THINKING,
I'M THINKING.
VERY WELL. I ACCEPT YOUR DEAL.
THE CHILDREN SHALL ACCOMPANY US ON OUR TRIP.
WITH YOU I LEAVE TANNGRISNIR AND TANNGNJOSTR, WHO ARE AS CLOSE TO ME AS YOUR CHILDREN ARE TO YOU.
I TRUST NO FURTHER HARM WILL COME TO THEM. LIKEWISE, YOU CAN KNOW YOUR CHILDREN ARE SAFE WITH US GODS.
POPPY?
YOU ARE IN SAFE HANDS, LITTLE ONE. I WILL BE HERE WHEN YOU RETURN.

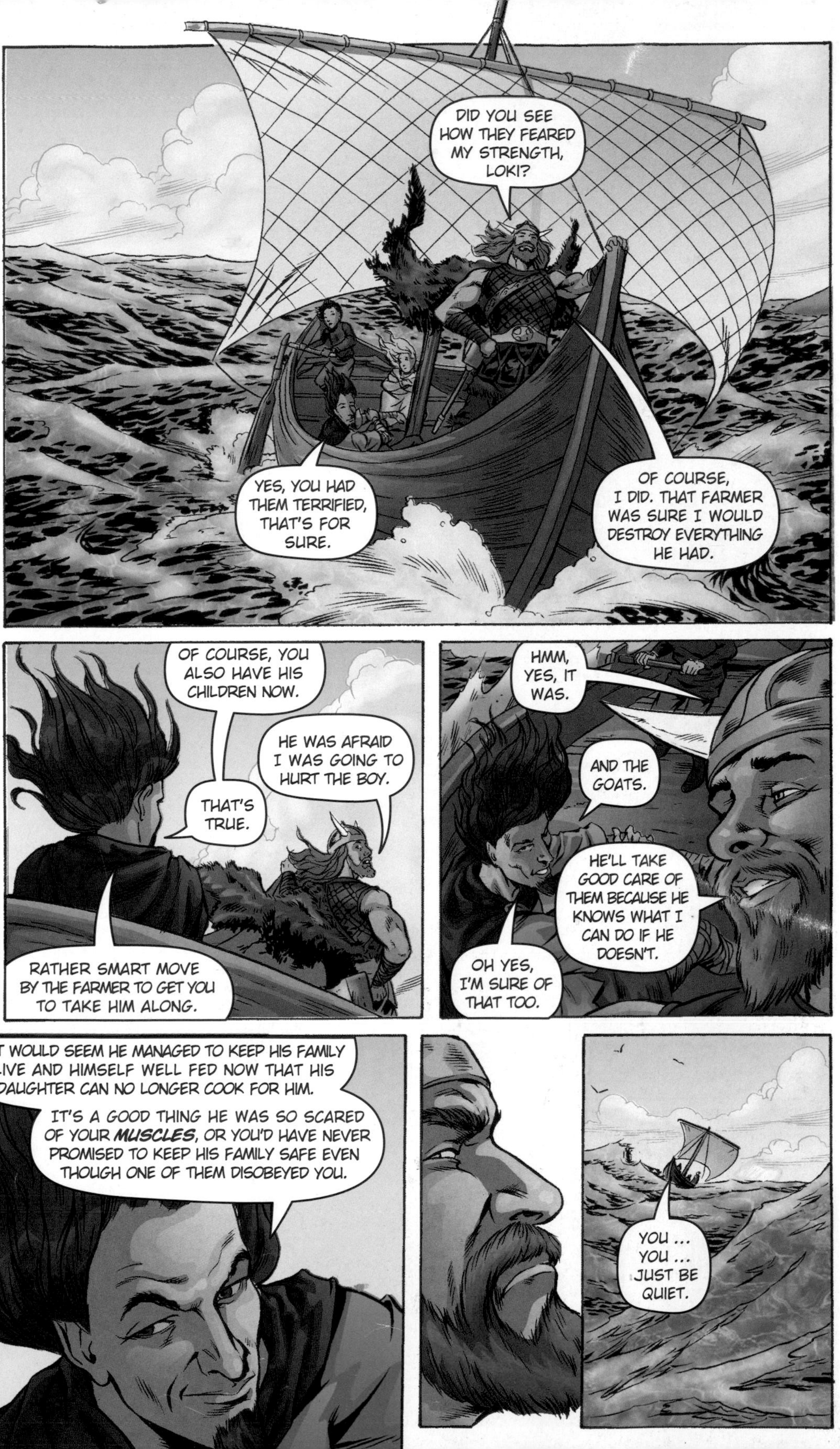
DID YOU SEE HOW THEY FEARED MY STRENGTH, LOKI?
YES, YOU HAD THEM TERRIFIED, THAT'S FOR SURE.
OF COURSE, I DID. THAT FARMER WAS SURE I WOULD DESTROY EVERYTHING HE HAD.
OF COURSE, YOU ALSO HAVE HIS CHILDREN NOW.
HE WAS AFRAID I WAS GOING TO HURT THE BOY.
THAT'S TRUE.
RATHER SMART MOVE BY THE FARMER TO GET YOU TO TAKE HIM ALONG.
HMM, YES, IT WAS.
AND THE GOATS.
HE'LL TAKE GOOD CARE OF THEM BECAUSE HE KNOWS WHAT I CAN DO IF HE DOESN'T.
OH YES, I'M SURE OF THAT TOO.
SO IT WOULD SEEM HE MANAGED TO KEEP HIS FAMILY ALIVE AND HIMSELF WELL FED NOW THAT HIS DAUGHTER CAN NO LONGER COOK FOR HIM.
IT'S A GOOD THING HE WAS SO SCARED OF YOUR *MUSCLES*, OR YOU'D HAVE NEVER PROMISED TO KEEP HIS FAMILY SAFE EVEN THOUGH ONE OF THEM DISOBEYED YOU.
YOU ... YOU ... JUST BE QUIET.

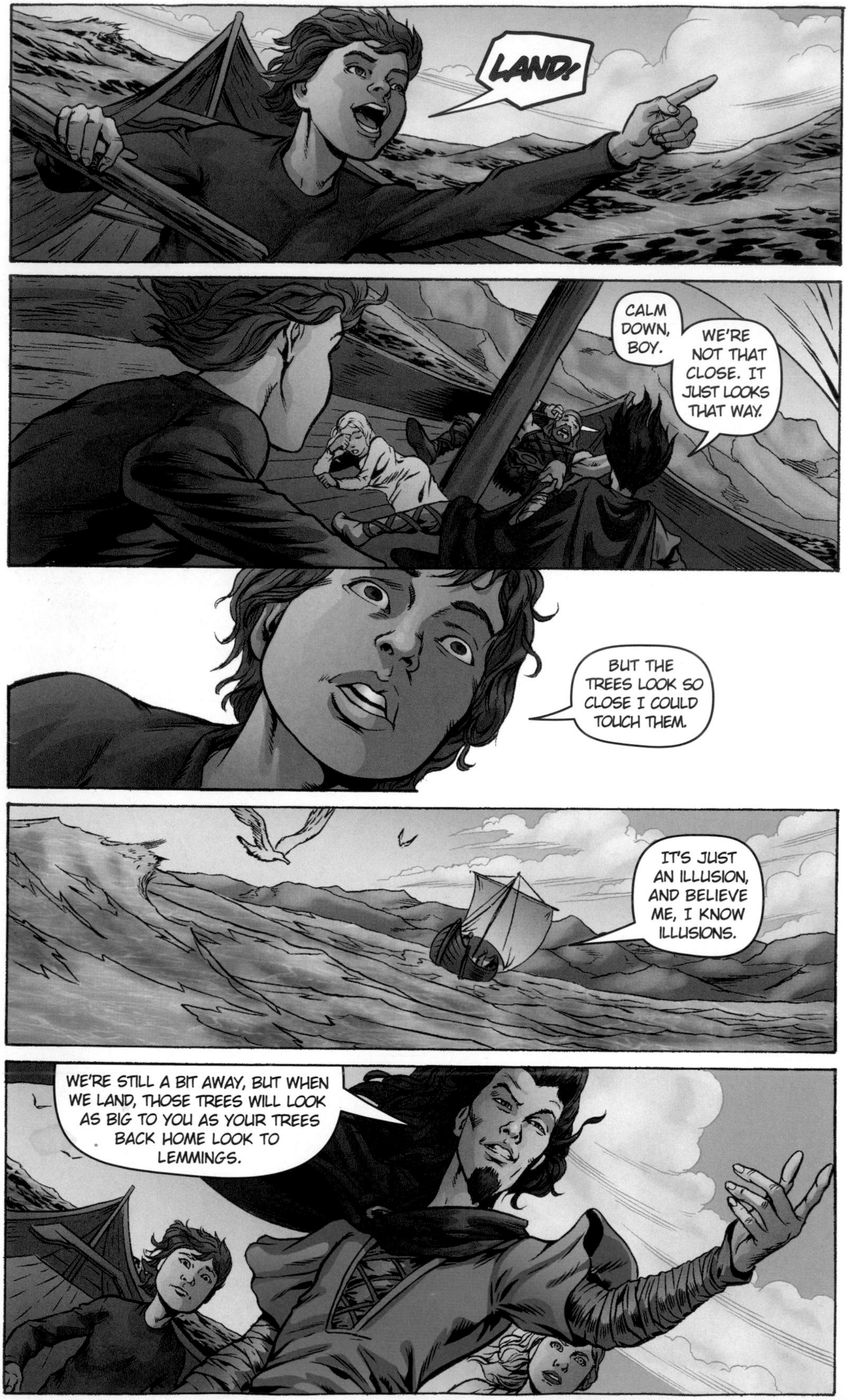
LAND!
CALM DOWN, BOY.
WE'RE NOT THAT CLOSE. IT JUST LOOKS THAT WAY.
BUT THE TREES LOOK SO CLOSE I COULD TOUCH THEM.
IT'S JUST AN ILLUSION, AND BELIEVE ME, I KNOW ILLUSIONS.
WE'RE STILL A BIT AWAY, BUT WHEN WE LAND, THOSE TREES WILL LOOK AS BIG TO YOU AS YOUR TREES BACK HOME LOOK TO LEMMINGS.

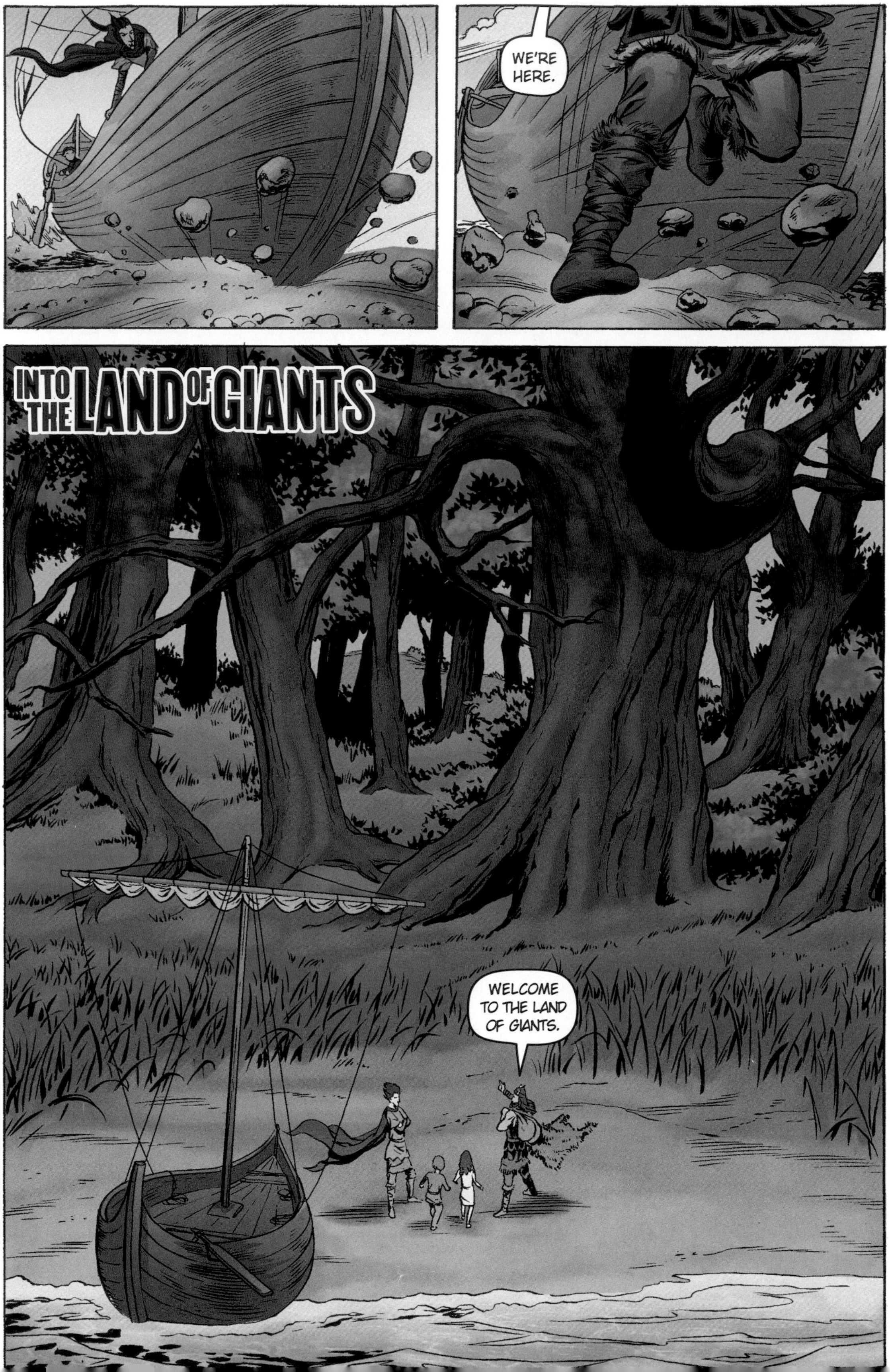
WE'RE HERE.
INTO THE LAND OF GIANTS
WELCOME TO THE LAND OF GIANTS.

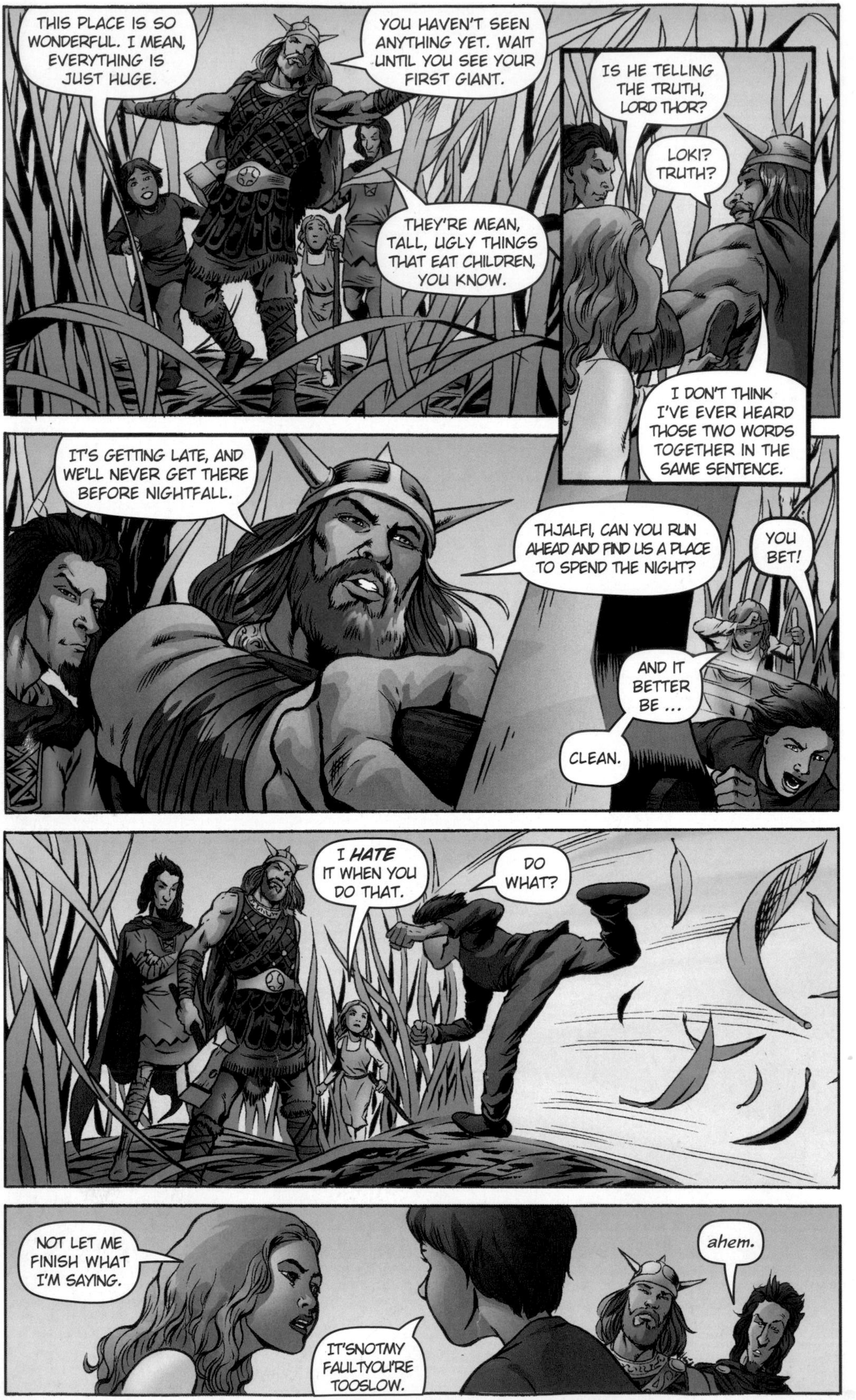
THIS PLACE IS SO WONDERFUL. I MEAN, EVERYTHING IS JUST HUGE.
YOU HAVEN'T SEEN ANYTHING YET. WAIT UNTIL YOU SEE YOUR FIRST GIANT.
THEY'RE MEAN, TALL, UGLY THINGS THAT EAT CHILDREN, YOU KNOW.
IS HE TELLING THE TRUTH, LORD THOR?
LOKI? TRUTH?
I DON'T THINK I'VE EVER HEARD THOSE TWO WORDS TOGETHER IN THE SAME SENTENCE.
IT'S GETTING LATE, AND WE'LL NEVER GET THERE BEFORE NIGHTFALL.
THJALFI, CAN YOU RUN AHEAD AND FIND US A PLACE TO SPEND THE NIGHT?
YOU BET!
AND IT BETTER BE ...
CLEAN.
I HATE IT WHEN YOU DO THAT.
DO WHAT?
NOT LET ME FINISH WHAT I'M SAYING.
IT'SNOTMY FAULTYOU'RE TOOSLOW.
ahem.

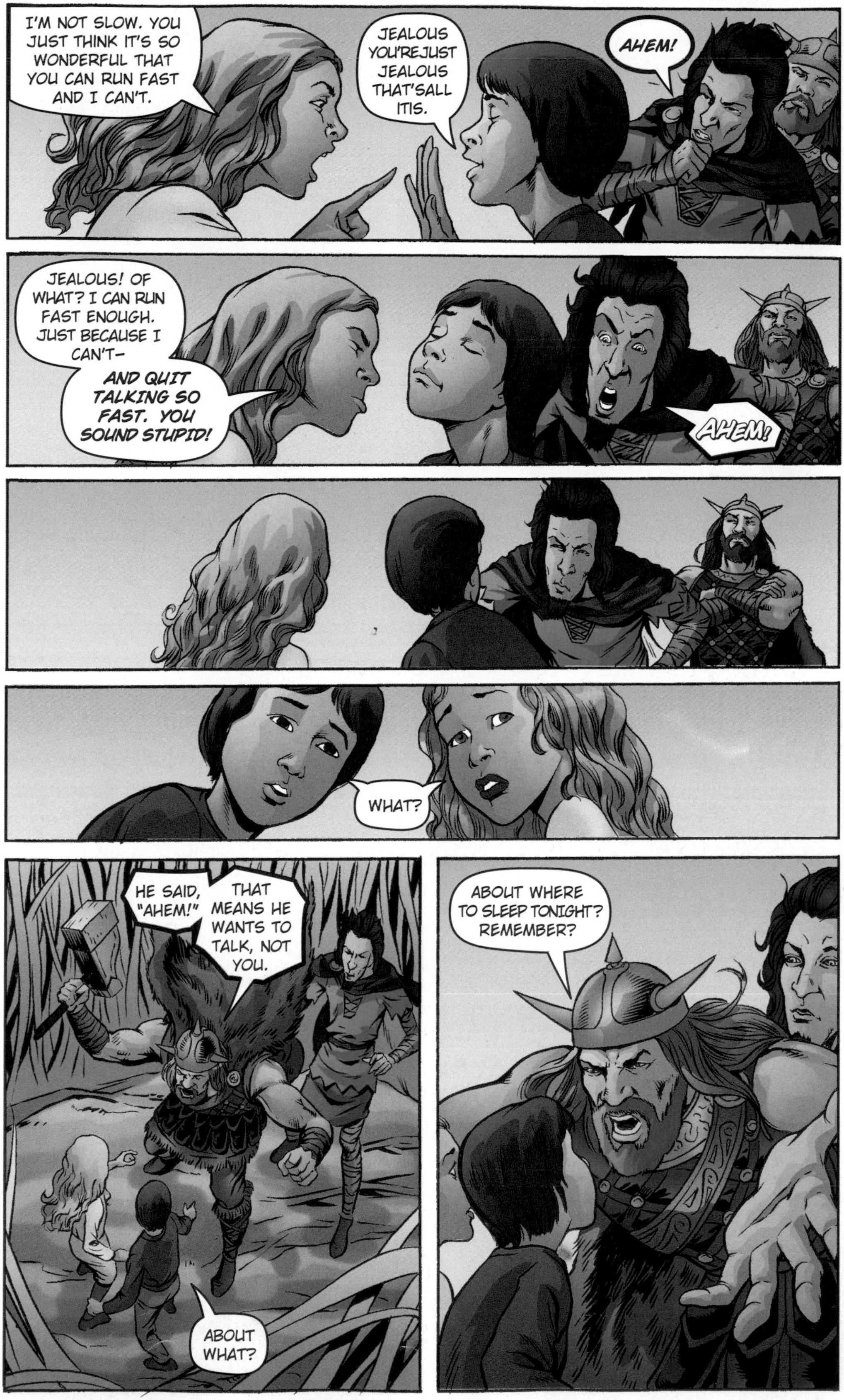
I'M NOT SLOW. YOU JUST THINK IT'S SO WONDERFUL THAT YOU CAN RUN FAST AND I CAN'T.
JEALOUS YOU'REJUST JEALOUS THAT'SALL ITIS.
AHEM!
JEALOUS! OF WHAT? I CAN RUN FAST ENOUGH. JUST BECAUSE I CAN'T—
AND QUIT TALKING SO FAST. YOU SOUND STUPID!
AHEM!
WHAT?
HE SAID, "AHEM!"
THAT MEANS HE WANTS TO TALK, NOT YOU.
ABOUT WHAT?
ABOUT WHERE TO SLEEP TONIGHT? REMEMBER?

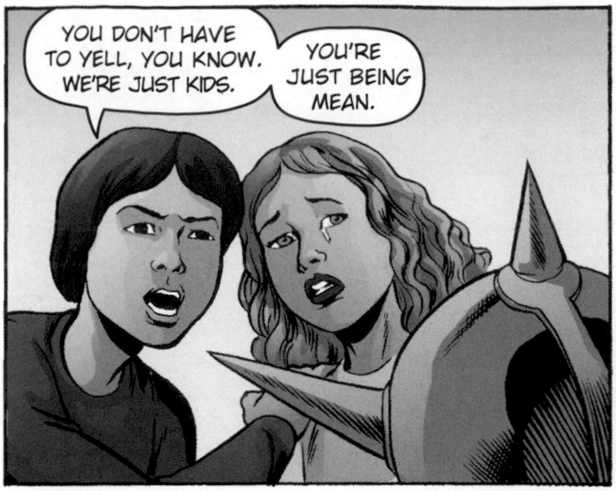
YOU DON'T HAVE TO YELL, YOU KNOW. WE'RE JUST KIDS.
YOU'RE JUST BEING MEAN.

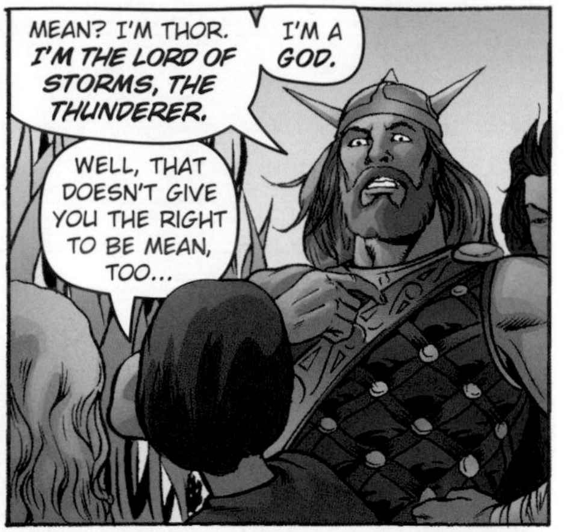
MEAN? I'M THOR. I'M THE LORD OF STORMS, THE THUNDERER.
I'M A GOD.
WELL, THAT DOESN'T GIVE YOU THE RIGHT TO BE MEAN, TOO...

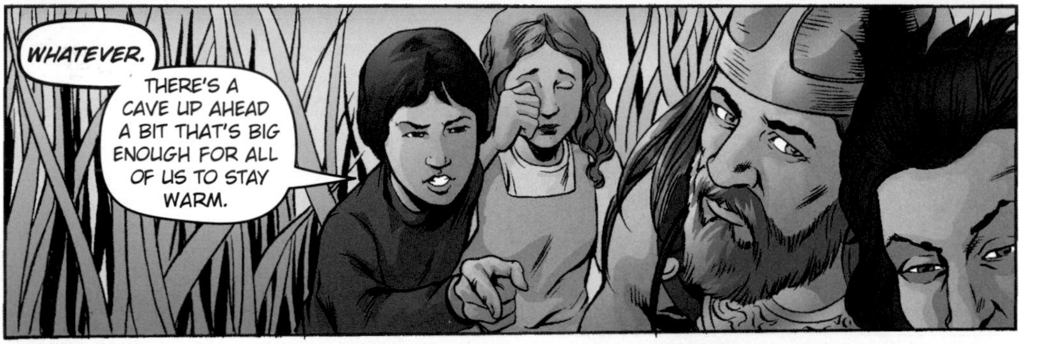
WHATEVER.
THERE'S A CAVE UP AHEAD A BIT THAT'S BIG ENOUGH FOR ALL OF US TO STAY WARM.

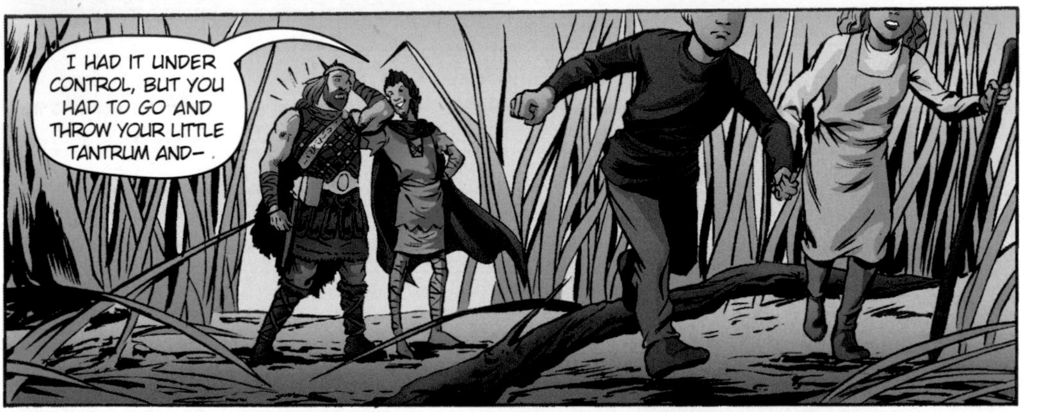
I HAD IT UNDER CONTROL, BUT YOU HAD TO GO AND THROW YOUR LITTLE TANTRUM AND-

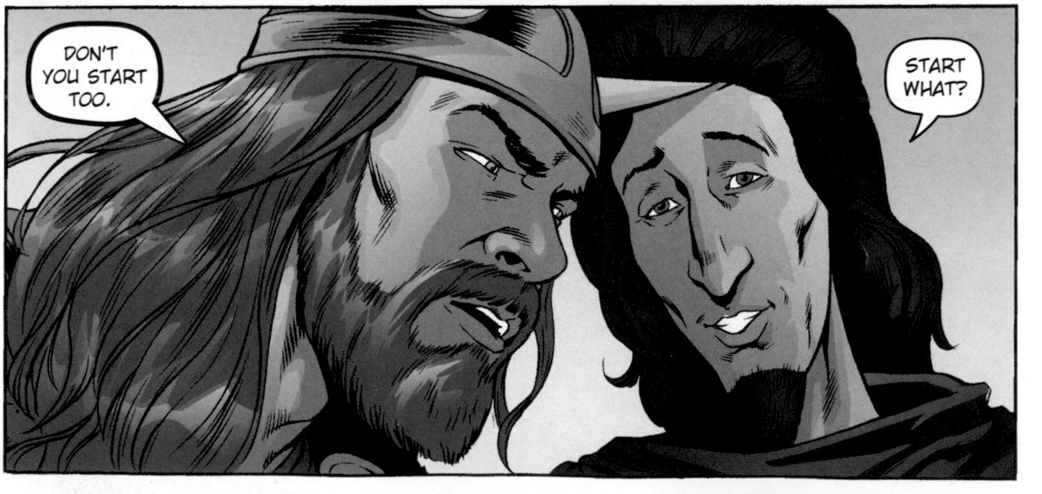
DON'T YOU START TOO.
START WHAT?

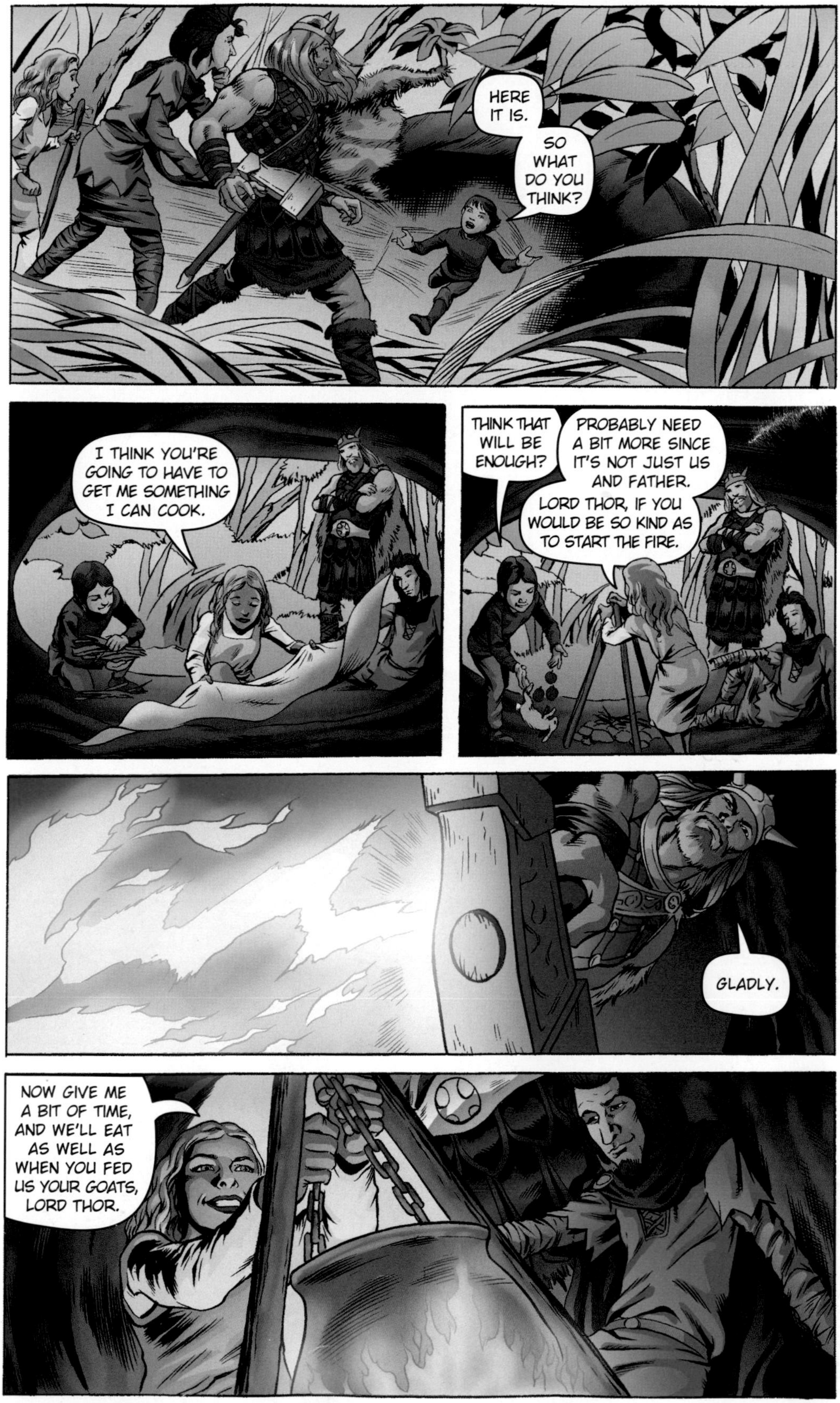
HERE IT IS.
SO WHAT DO YOU THINK?
I THINK YOU'RE GOING TO HAVE TO GET ME SOMETHING I CAN COOK.
THINK THAT WILL BE ENOUGH?
PROBABLY NEED A BIT MORE SINCE IT'S NOT JUST US AND FATHER.
LORD THOR, IF YOU WOULD BE SO KIND AS TO START THE FIRE.
GLADLY.
NOW GIVE ME A BIT OF TIME, AND WE'LL EAT AS WELL AS WHEN YOU FED US YOUR GOATS, LORD THOR.

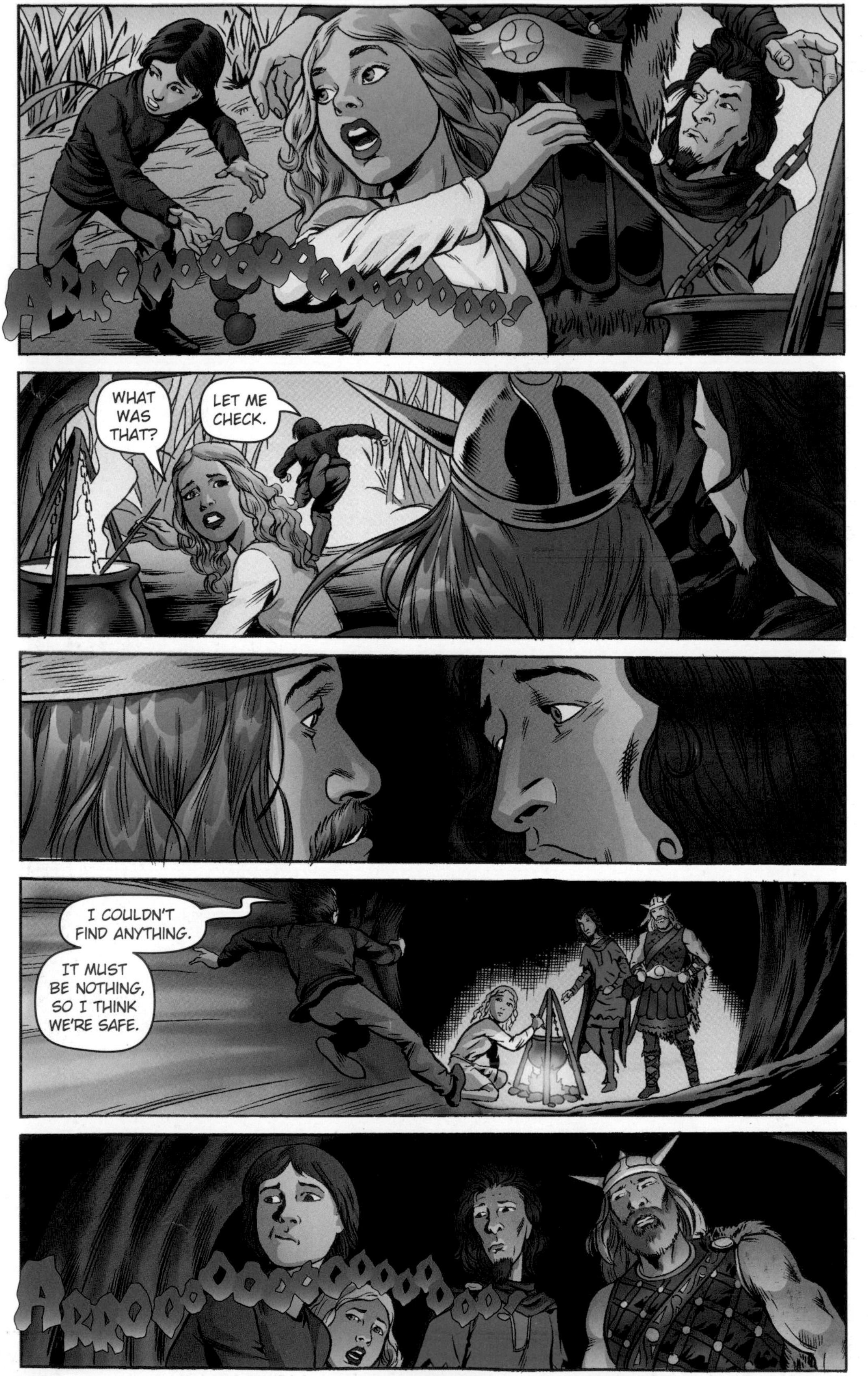
ARROOOOOOOOOOOOOOOOOO!
WHAT WAS THAT?
LET ME CHECK.
I COULDN'T FIND ANYTHING.
IT MUST BE NOTHING, SO I THINK WE'RE SAFE.
ARROOOOOOOOOOOOOOOOOO!

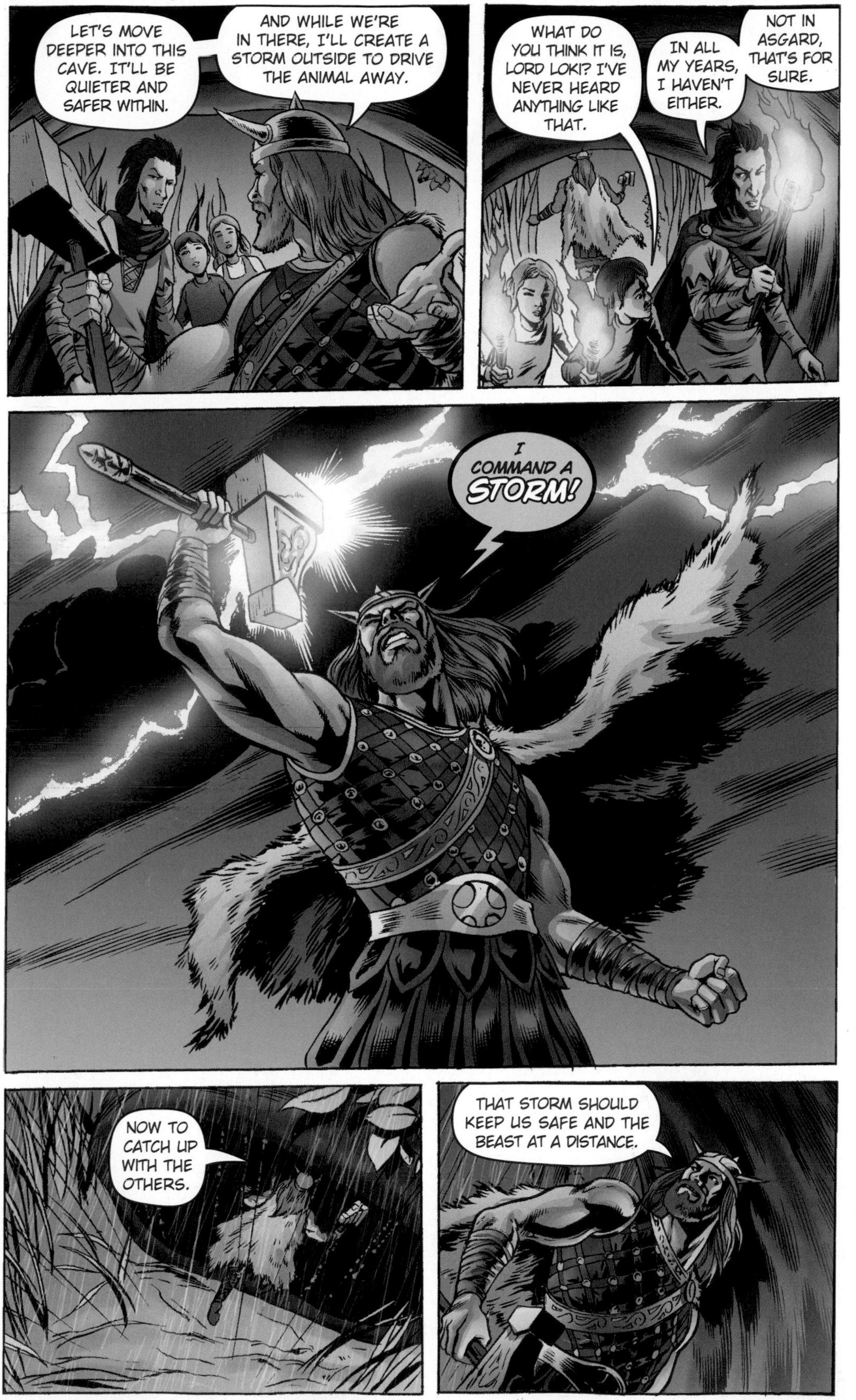
LET'S MOVE DEEPER INTO THIS CAVE. IT'LL BE QUIETER AND SAFER WITHIN.
AND WHILE WE'RE IN THERE, I'LL CREATE A STORM OUTSIDE TO DRIVE THE ANIMAL AWAY.
WHAT DO YOU THINK IT IS, LORD LOKI? I'VE NEVER HEARD ANYTHING LIKE THAT.
IN ALL MY YEARS, I HAVEN'T EITHER.
NOT IN ASGARD, THAT'S FOR SURE.
I COMMAND A STORM!
NOW TO CATCH UP WITH THE OTHERS.
THAT STORM SHOULD KEEP US SAFE AND THE BEAST AT A DISTANCE.

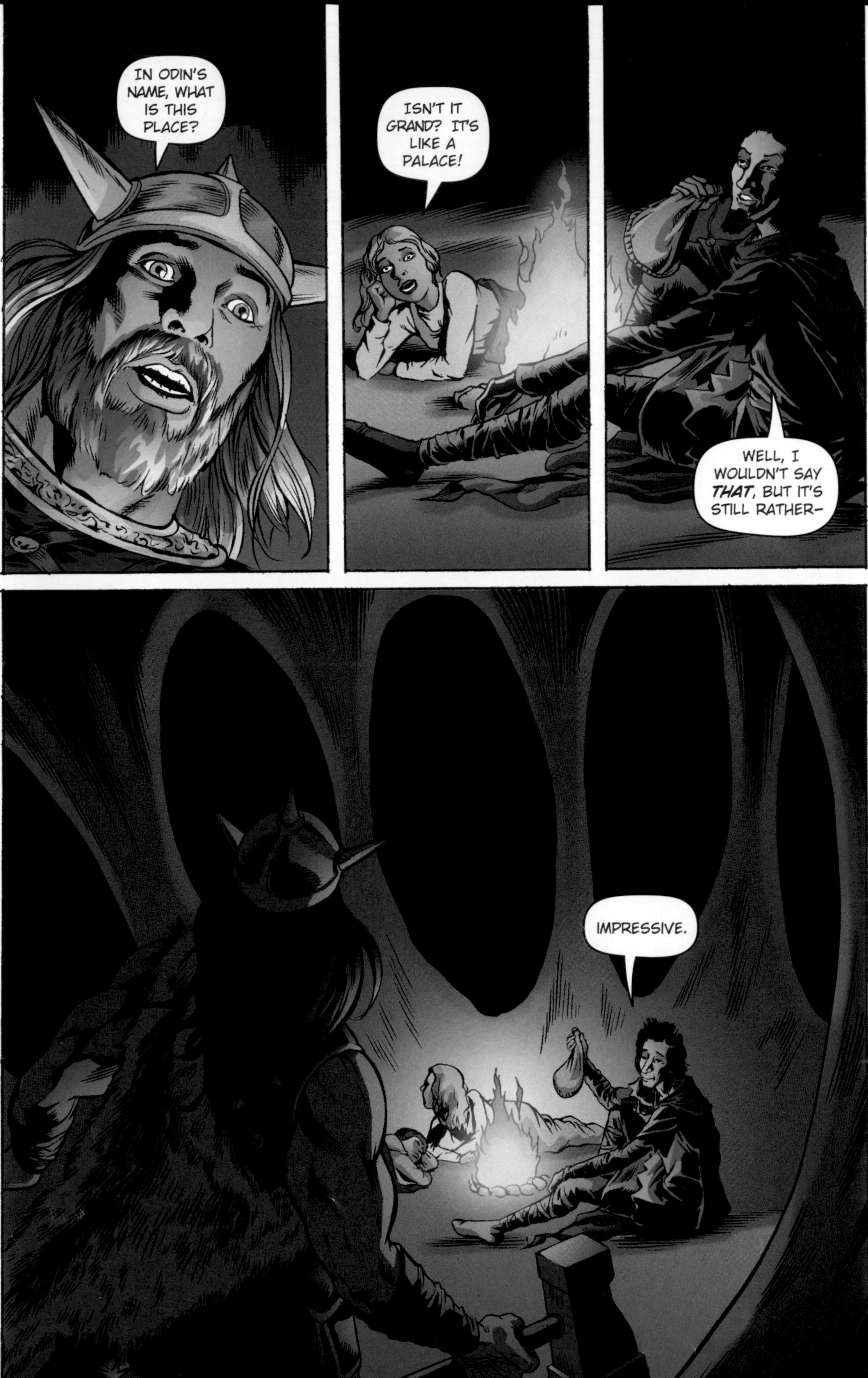
IN ODIN'S NAME, WHAT IS THIS PLACE?
ISN'T IT GRAND? IT'S LIKE A PALACE!
WELL, I WOULDN'T SAY *THAT*, BUT IT'S STILL RATHER-
IMPRESSIVE.

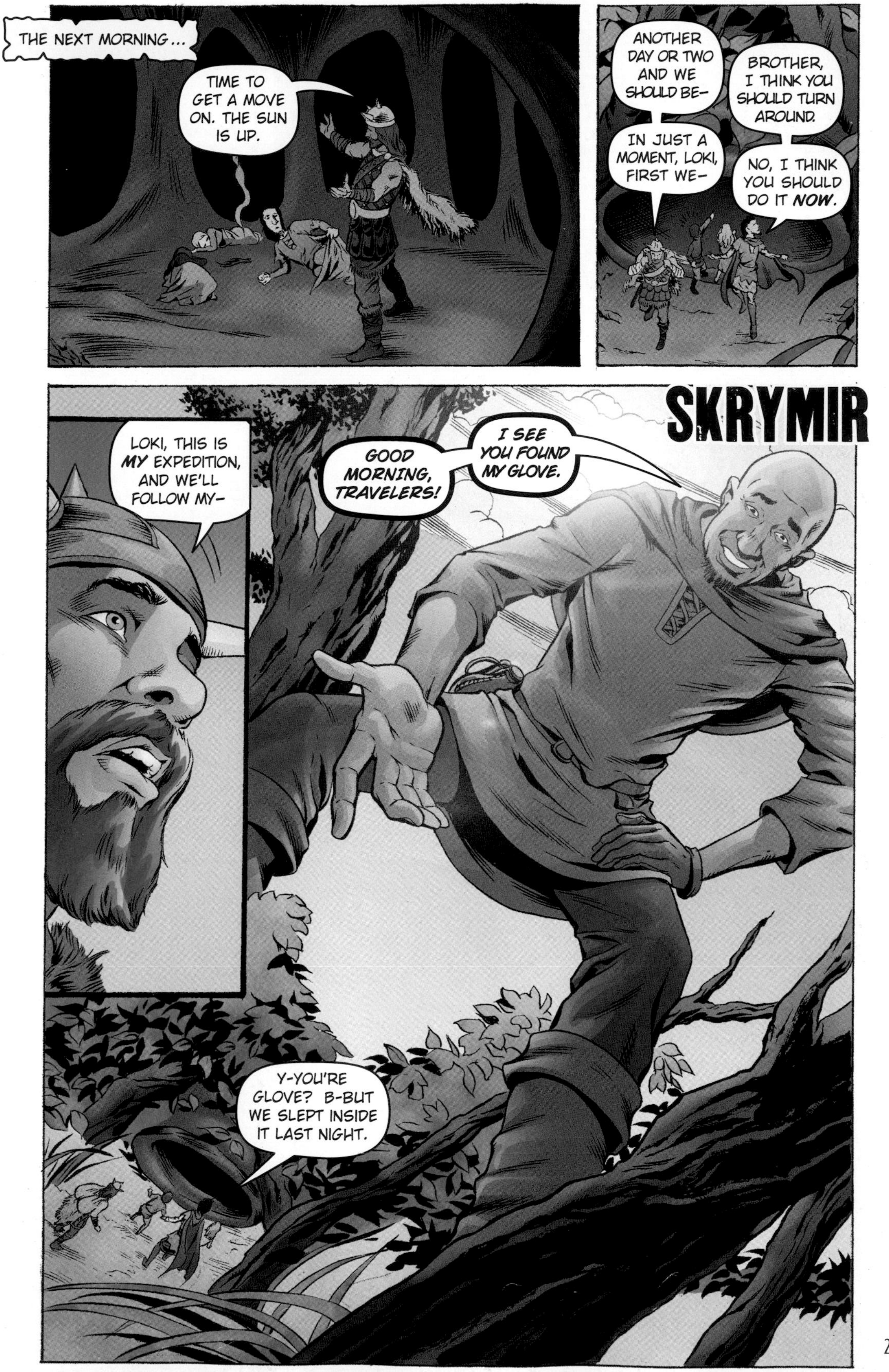
THE NEXT MORNING...
TIME TO GET A MOVE ON. THE SUN IS UP.
ANOTHER DAY OR TWO AND WE SHOULD BE-
BROTHER, I THINK YOU SHOULD TURN AROUND.
IN JUST A MOMENT, LOKI, FIRST WE-
NO, I THINK YOU SHOULD DO IT NOW.
SKRYMIR
LOKI, THIS IS MY EXPEDITION, AND WE'LL FOLLOW MY-
GOOD MORNING, TRAVELERS!
I SEE YOU FOUND MY GLOVE.
Y-YOU'RE GLOVE? B-BUT WE SLEPT INSIDE IT LAST NIGHT.

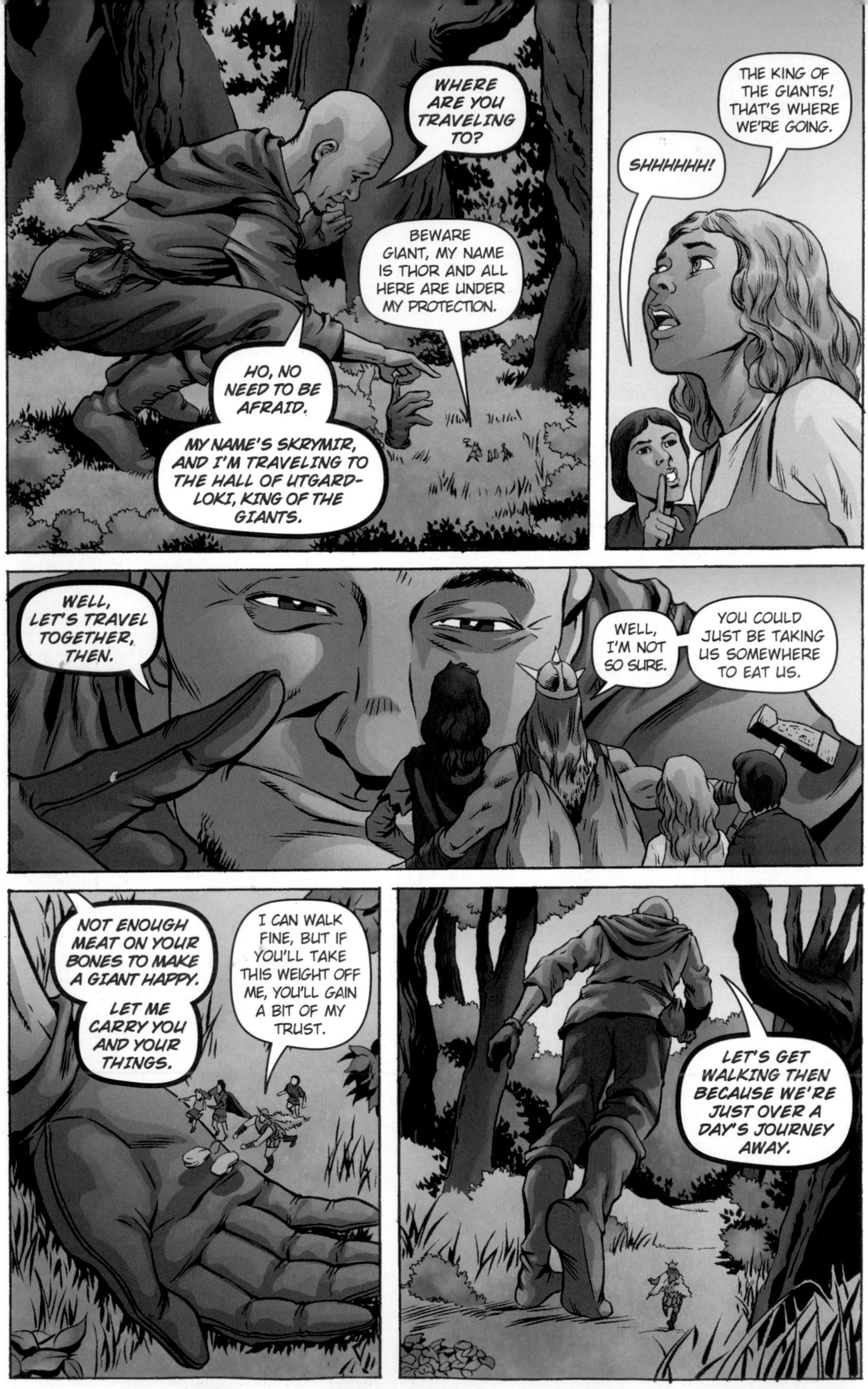
WHERE ARE YOU TRAVELING TO?
BEWARE GIANT, MY NAME IS THOR AND ALL HERE ARE UNDER MY PROTECTION.
HO, NO NEED TO BE AFRAID.
MY NAME'S SKRYMIR, AND I'M TRAVELING TO THE HALL OF UTGARD-LOKI, KING OF THE GIANTS.
THE KING OF THE GIANTS! THAT'S WHERE WE'RE GOING.
SHHHHHH!
WELL, LET'S TRAVEL TOGETHER, THEN.
WELL, I'M NOT SO SURE.
YOU COULD JUST BE TAKING US SOMEWHERE TO EAT US.
NOT ENOUGH MEAT ON YOUR BONES TO MAKE A GIANT HAPPY.
LET ME CARRY YOU AND YOUR THINGS.
I CAN WALK FINE, BUT IF YOU'LL TAKE THIS WEIGHT OFF ME, YOU'LL GAIN A BIT OF MY TRUST.
LET'S GET WALKING THEN BECAUSE WE'RE JUST OVER A DAY'S JOURNEY AWAY.

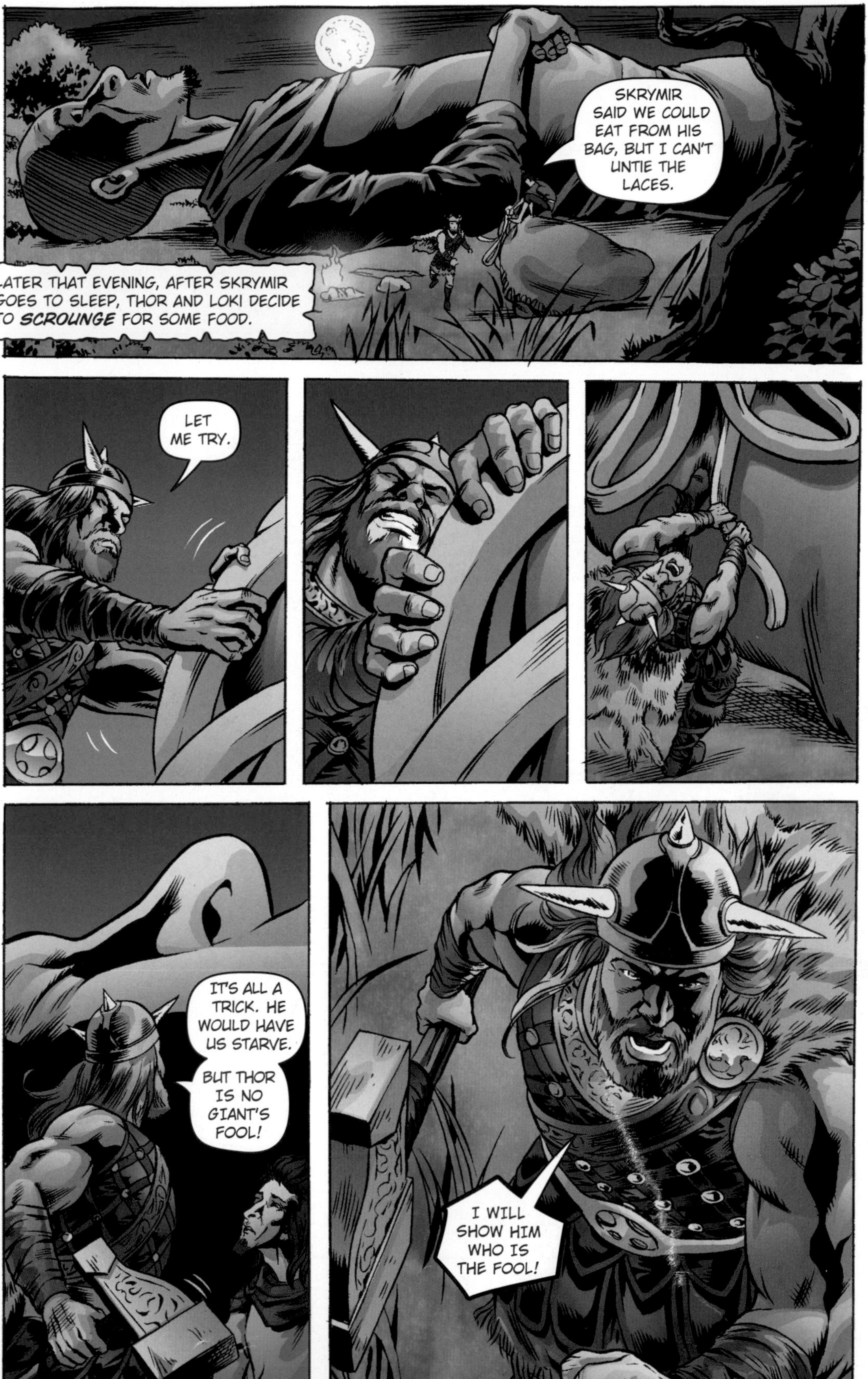
SKRYMIR SAID WE COULD EAT FROM HIS BAG, BUT I CAN'T UNTIE THE LACES.
LATER THAT EVENING, AFTER SKRYMIR GOES TO SLEEP, THOR AND LOKI DECIDE TO SCROUNGE FOR SOME FOOD.
LET ME TRY.
IT'S ALL A TRICK. HE WOULD HAVE US STARVE.
BUT THOR IS NO GIANT'S FOOL!
I WILL SHOW HIM WHO IS THE FOOL!

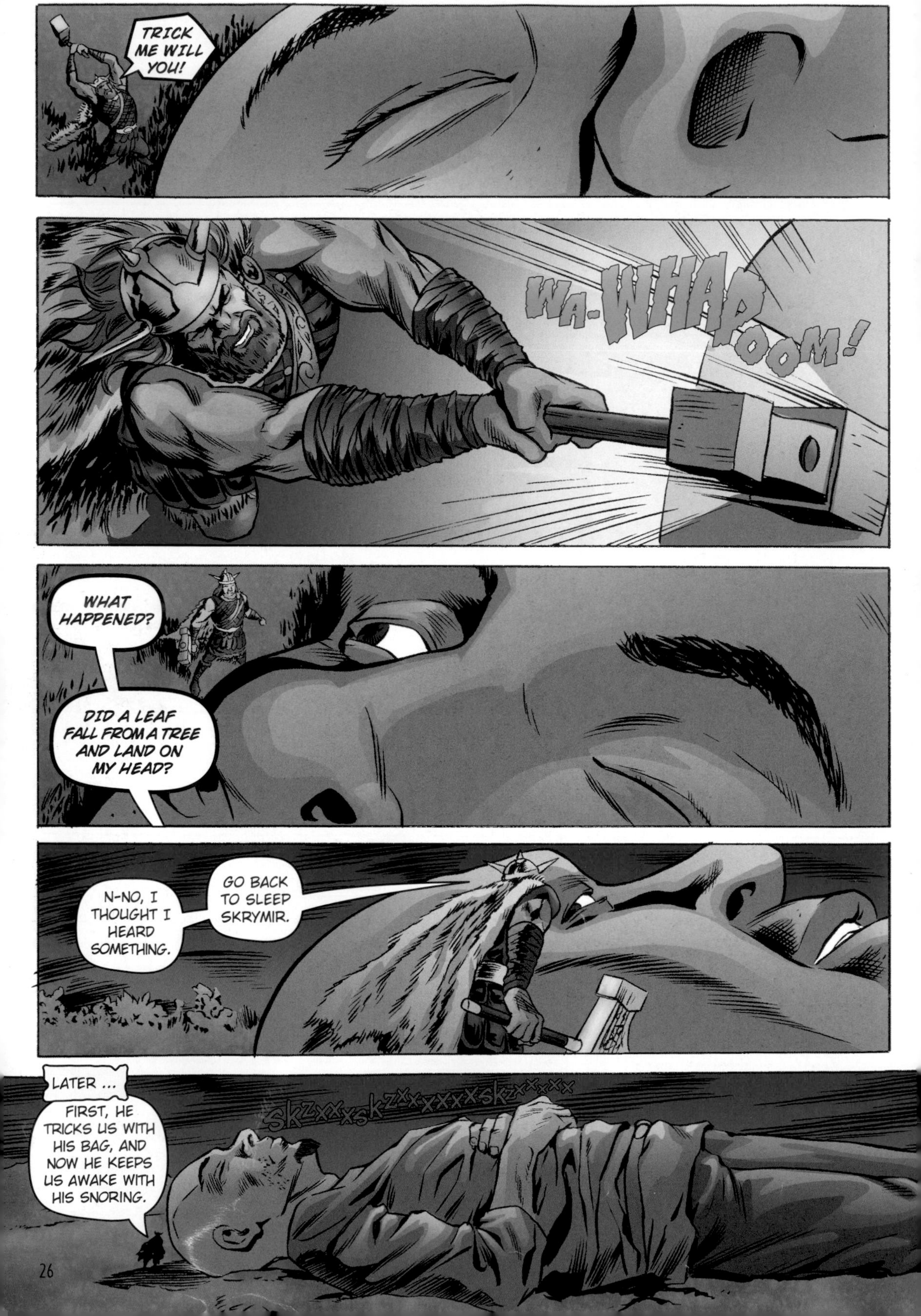
TRICK ME WILL YOU!
WA-WHAPOOM!
WHAT HAPPENED?
DID A LEAF FALL FROM A TREE AND LAND ON MY HEAD?
N-NO, I THOUGHT I HEARD SOMETHING.
GO BACK TO SLEEP SKRYMIR.
LATER ...
SKZXXXSKZXXXXXXSKZXXXX
FIRST, HE TRICKS US WITH HIS BAG, AND NOW HE KEEPS US AWAKE WITH HIS SNORING.

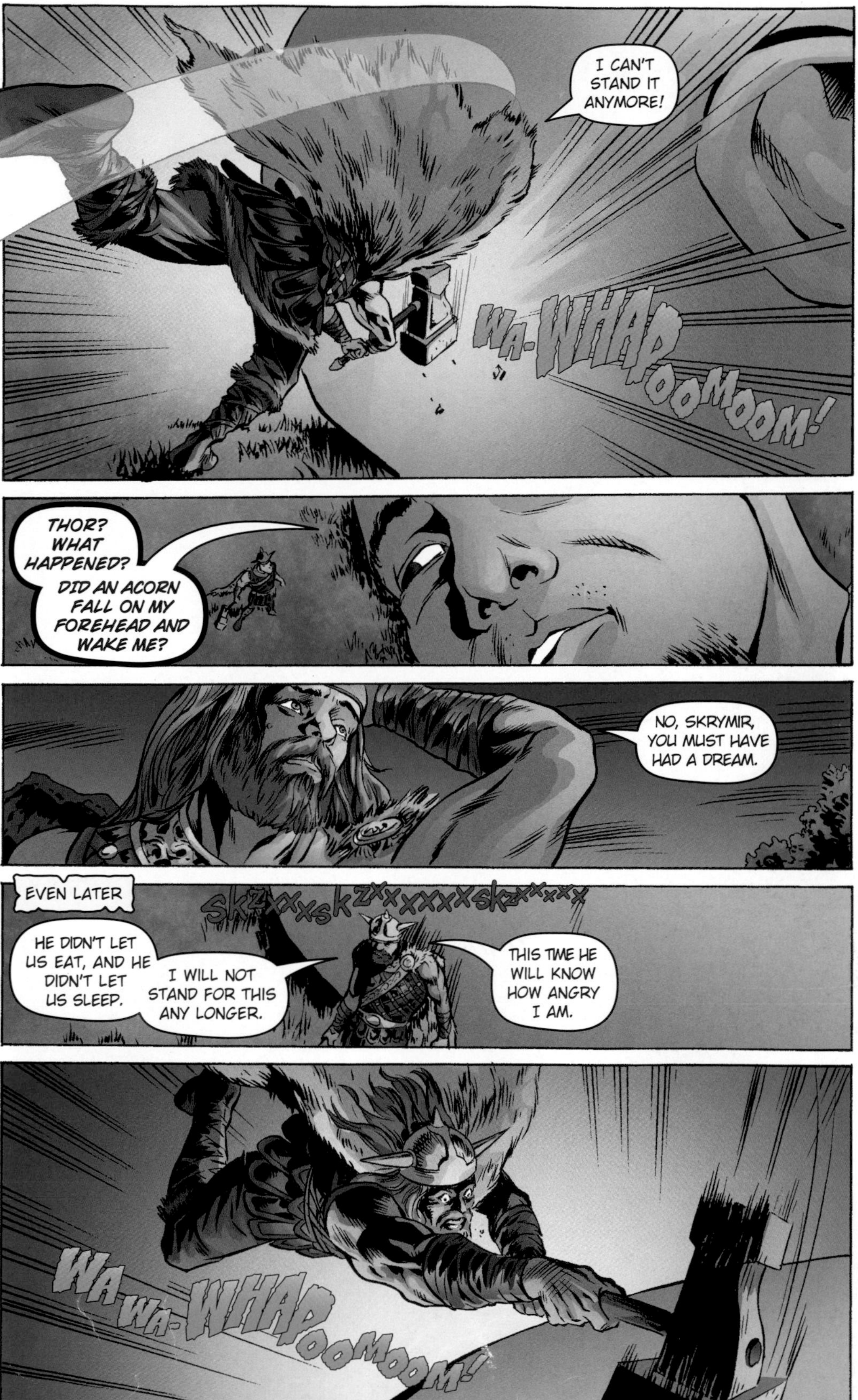
I CAN'T STAND IT ANYMORE!
WA-WHAPOOMOOM!
THOR? WHAT HAPPENED?
DID AN ACORN FALL ON MY FOREHEAD AND WAKE ME?
NO, SKRYMIR, YOU MUST HAVE HAD A DREAM.
EVEN LATER
SKZXXXSKZXXXXXXSKZXXXXX
HE DIDN'T LET US EAT, AND HE DIDN'T LET US SLEEP.
I WILL NOT STAND FOR THIS ANY LONGER.
THIS TIME HE WILL KNOW HOW ANGRY I AM.
WA WA-WHAPOOMOOM!

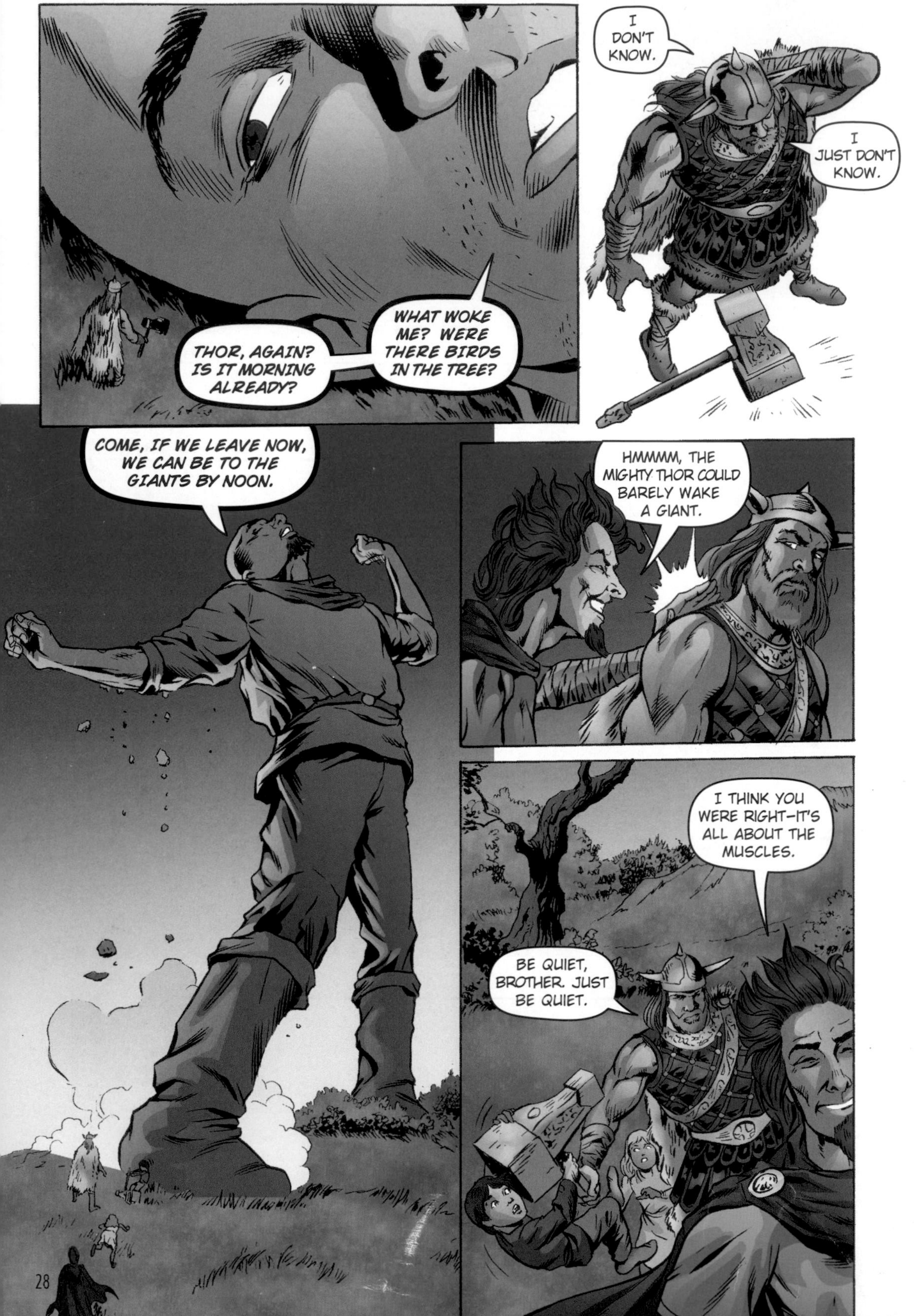
WHAT WOKE ME? WERE THERE BIRDS IN THE TREE?
THOR, AGAIN? IS IT MORNING ALREADY?
I DON'T KNOW.
I JUST DON'T KNOW.
COME, IF WE LEAVE NOW, WE CAN BE TO THE GIANTS BY NOON.
HMMMM, THE MIGHTY THOR COULD BARELY WAKE A GIANT.
I THINK YOU WERE RIGHT—IT'S ALL ABOUT THE MUSCLES.
BE QUIET, BROTHER. JUST BE QUIET.

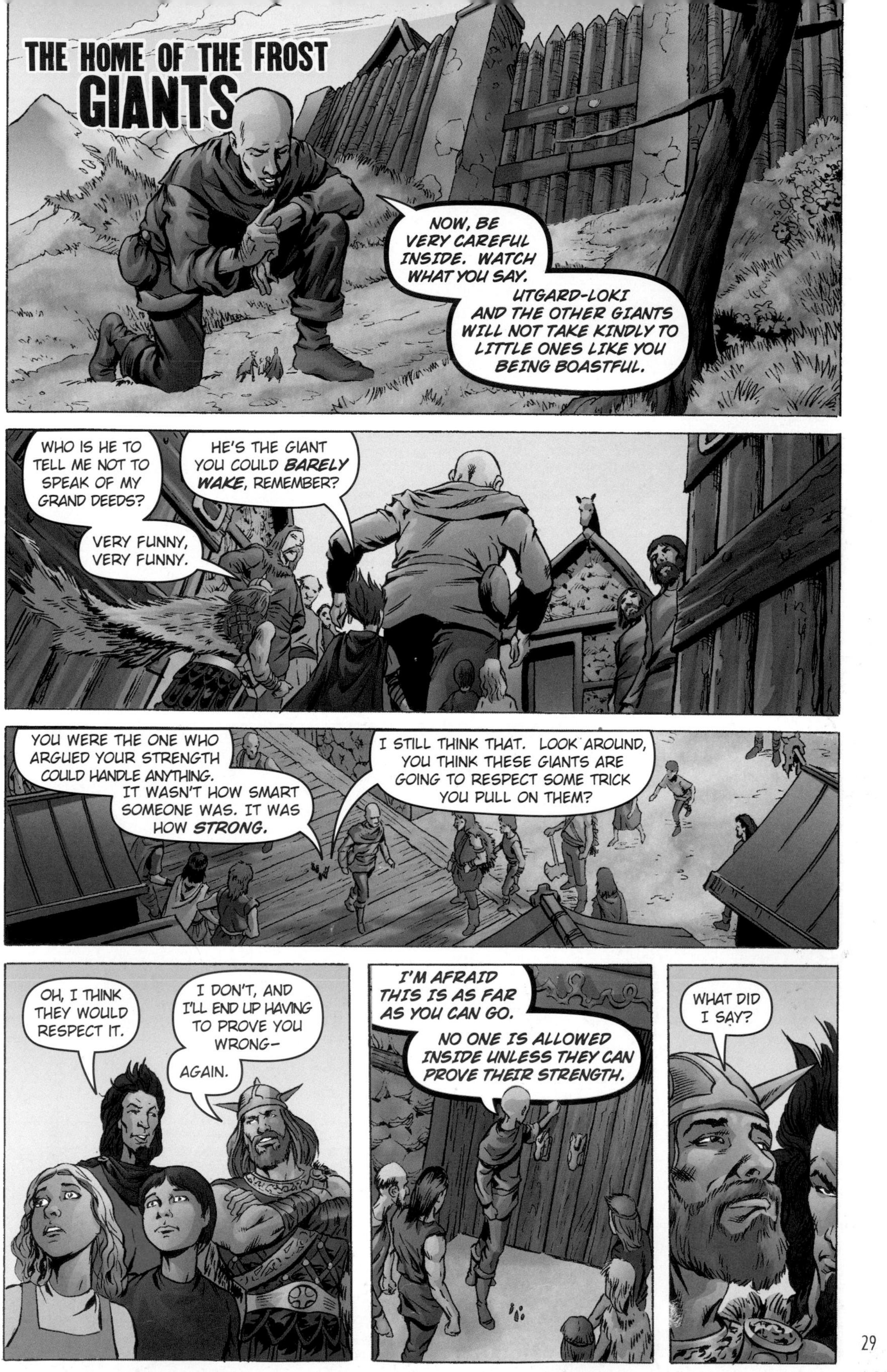
THE HOME OF THE FROST GIANTS
NOW, BE VERY CAREFUL INSIDE. WATCH WHAT YOU SAY.
UTGARD-LOKI AND THE OTHER GIANTS WILL NOT TAKE KINDLY TO LITTLE ONES LIKE YOU BEING BOASTFUL.
WHO IS HE TO TELL ME NOT TO SPEAK OF MY GRAND DEEDS?
HE'S THE GIANT YOU COULD BARELY WAKE, REMEMBER?
VERY FUNNY, VERY FUNNY.
YOU WERE THE ONE WHO ARGUED YOUR STRENGTH COULD HANDLE ANYTHING.
IT WASN'T HOW SMART SOMEONE WAS. IT WAS HOW STRONG.
I STILL THINK THAT. LOOK AROUND, YOU THINK THESE GIANTS ARE GOING TO RESPECT SOME TRICK YOU PULL ON THEM?
OH, I THINK THEY WOULD RESPECT IT.
I DON'T, AND I'LL END UP HAVING TO PROVE YOU WRONG-
AGAIN.
I'M AFRAID THIS IS AS FAR AS YOU CAN GO.
NO ONE IS ALLOWED INSIDE UNLESS THEY CAN PROVE THEIR STRENGTH.
WHAT DID I SAY?

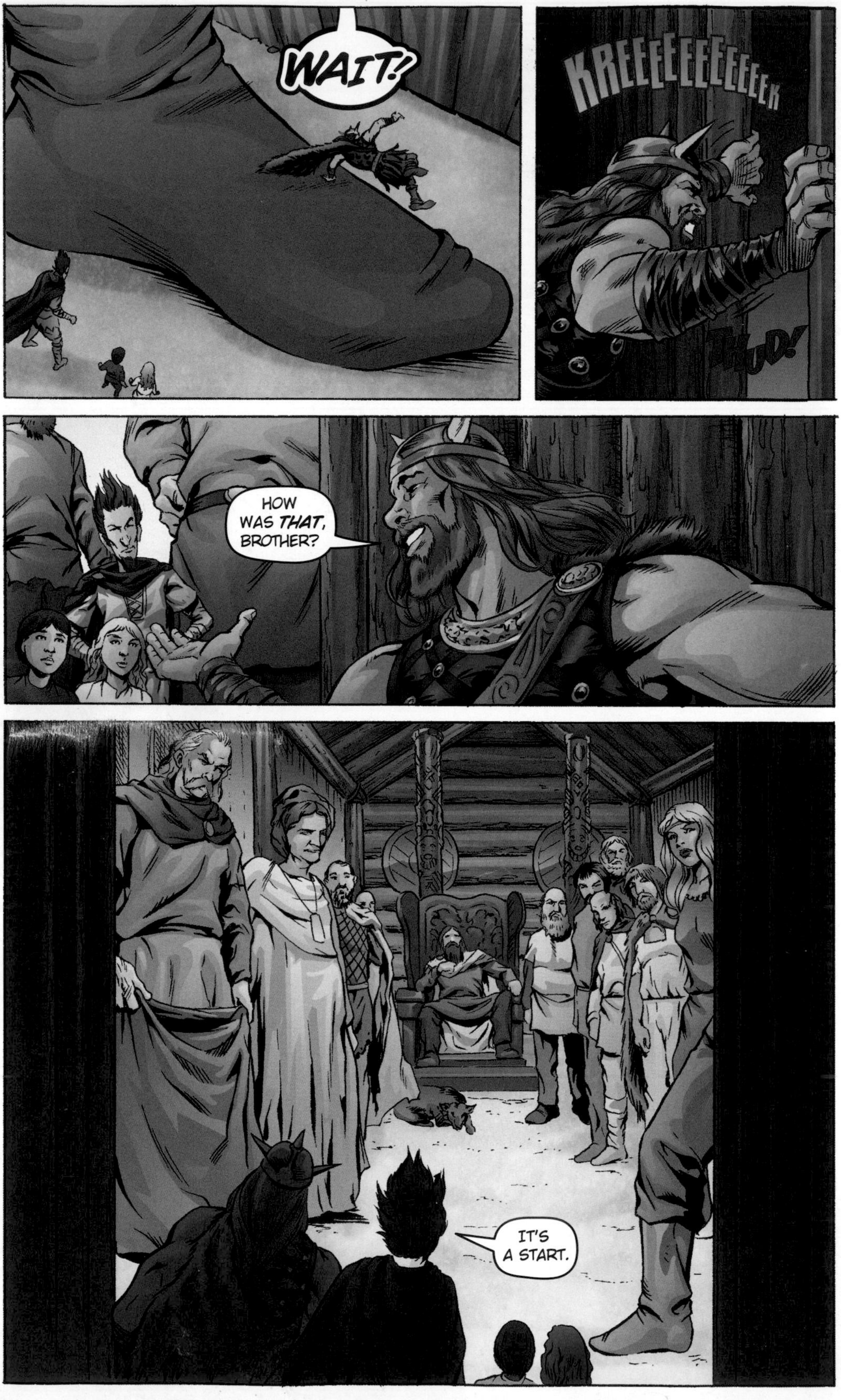
WAIT!
KREEEEEEEEEEEK
THUD!
HOW WAS *THAT*, BROTHER?
IT'S A START.

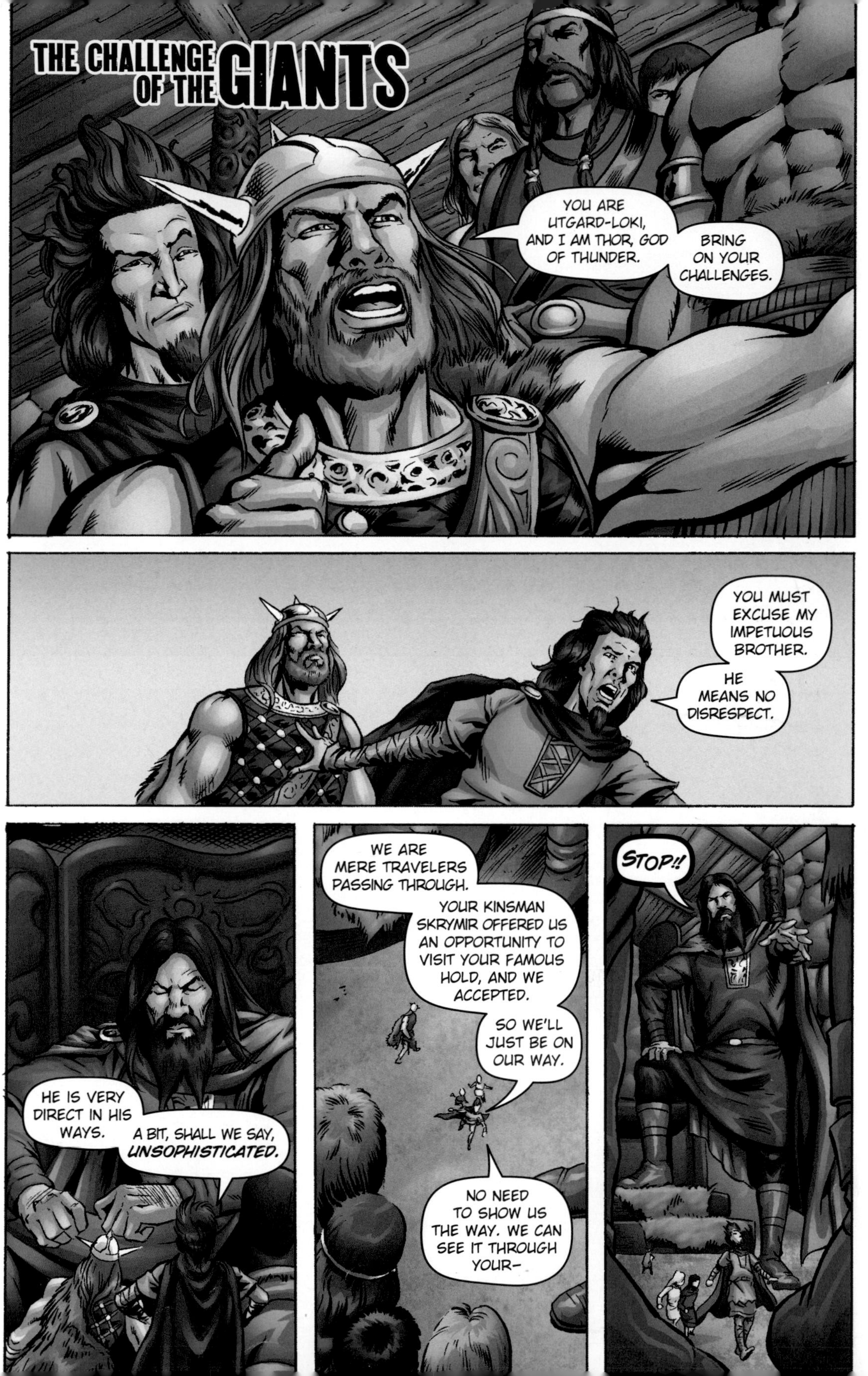
THE CHALLENGE OF THE GIANTS
YOU ARE UTGARD-LOKI, AND I AM THOR, GOD OF THUNDER.
BRING ON YOUR CHALLENGES.
YOU MUST EXCUSE MY IMPETUOUS BROTHER.
HE MEANS NO DISRESPECT.
HE IS VERY DIRECT IN HIS WAYS.
A BIT, SHALL WE SAY, *UNSOPHISTICATED.*
WE ARE MERE TRAVELERS PASSING THROUGH.
YOUR KINSMAN SKRYMIR OFFERED US AN OPPORTUNITY TO VISIT YOUR FAMOUS HOLD, AND WE ACCEPTED.
SO WE'LL JUST BE ON OUR WAY.
NO NEED TO SHOW US THE WAY. WE CAN SEE IT THROUGH YOUR–
STOP!!

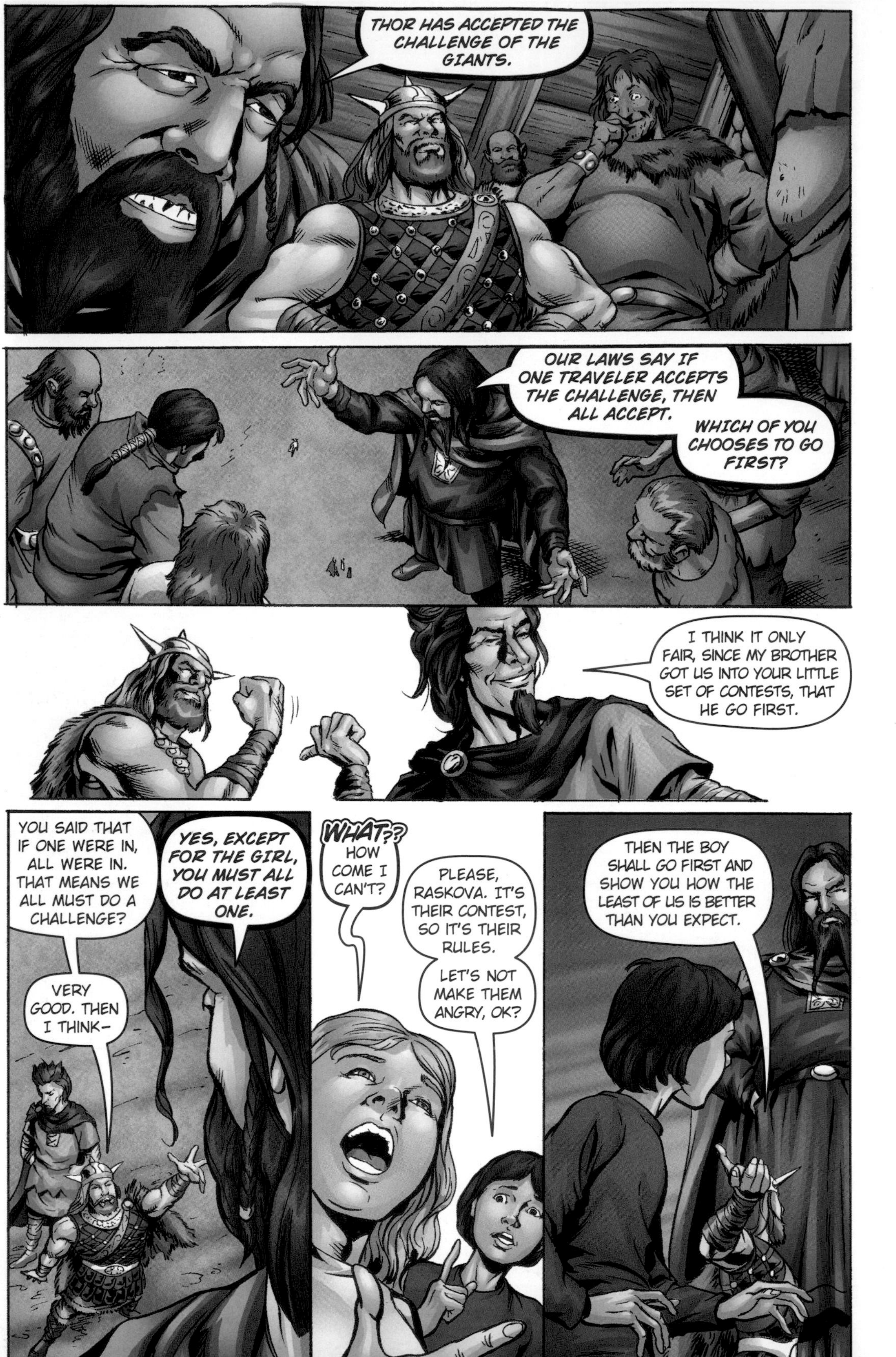
THOR HAS ACCEPTED THE CHALLENGE OF THE GIANTS.
OUR LAWS SAY IF ONE TRAVELER ACCEPTS THE CHALLENGE, THEN ALL ACCEPT.
WHICH OF YOU CHOOSES TO GO FIRST?
I THINK IT ONLY FAIR, SINCE MY BROTHER GOT US INTO YOUR LITTLE SET OF CONTESTS, THAT HE GO FIRST.
YOU SAID THAT IF ONE WERE IN, ALL WERE IN. THAT MEANS WE ALL MUST DO A CHALLENGE?
YES, EXCEPT FOR THE GIRL, YOU MUST ALL DO AT LEAST ONE.
VERY GOOD. THEN I THINK–
WHAT?? HOW COME I CAN'T?
PLEASE, RASKOVA. IT'S THEIR CONTEST, SO IT'S THEIR RULES.
LET'S NOT MAKE THEM ANGRY, OK?
THEN THE BOY SHALL GO FIRST AND SHOW YOU HOW THE LEAST OF US IS BETTER THAN YOU EXPECT.

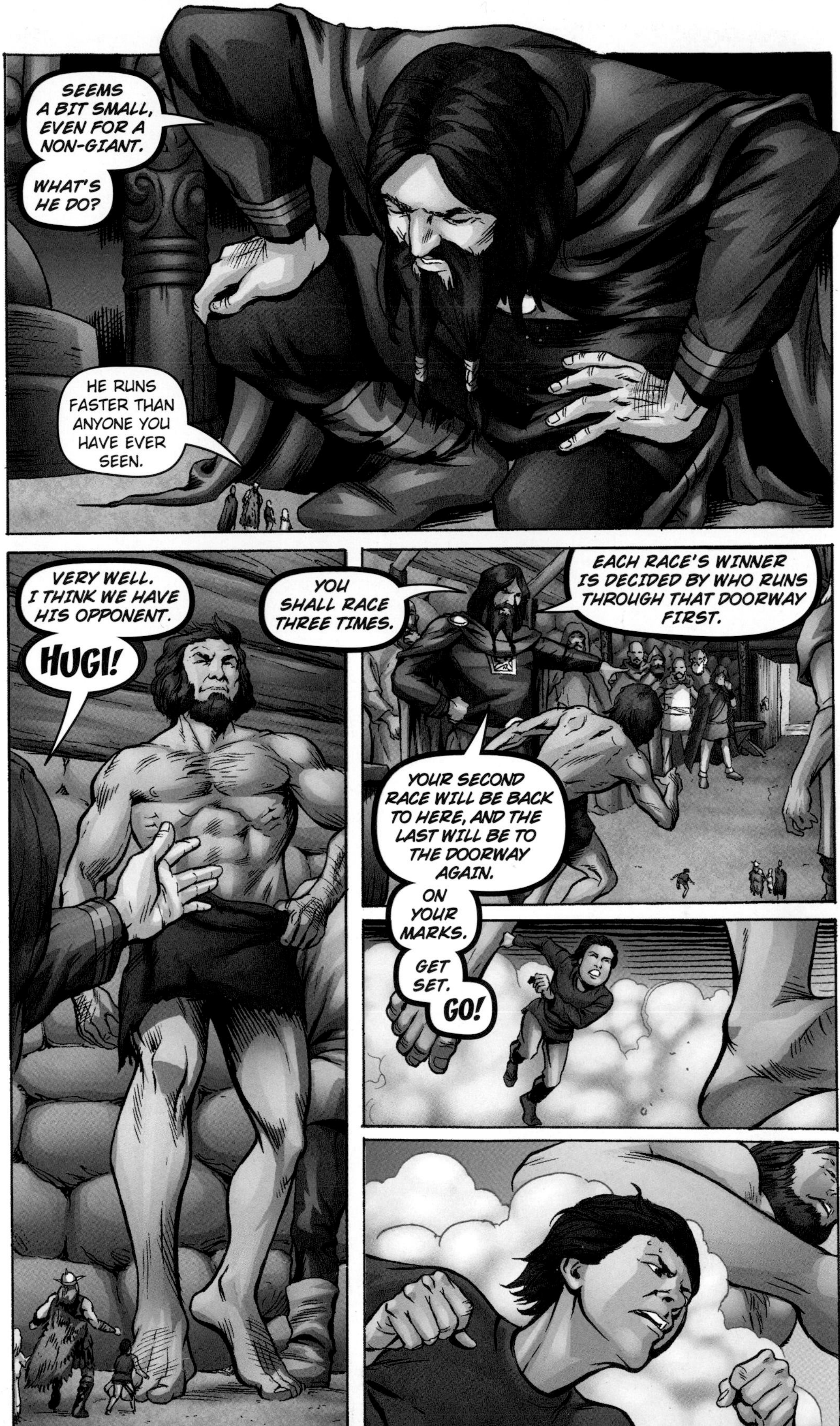
SEEMS A BIT SMALL, EVEN FOR A NON-GIANT.
WHAT'S HE DO?
HE RUNS FASTER THAN ANYONE YOU HAVE EVER SEEN.
VERY WELL. I THINK WE HAVE HIS OPPONENT.
HUGI!
YOU SHALL RACE THREE TIMES.
EACH RACE'S WINNER IS DECIDED BY WHO RUNS THROUGH THAT DOORWAY FIRST.
YOUR SECOND RACE WILL BE BACK TO HERE, AND THE LAST WILL BE TO THE DOORWAY AGAIN.
ON YOUR MARKS.
GET SET.
GO!

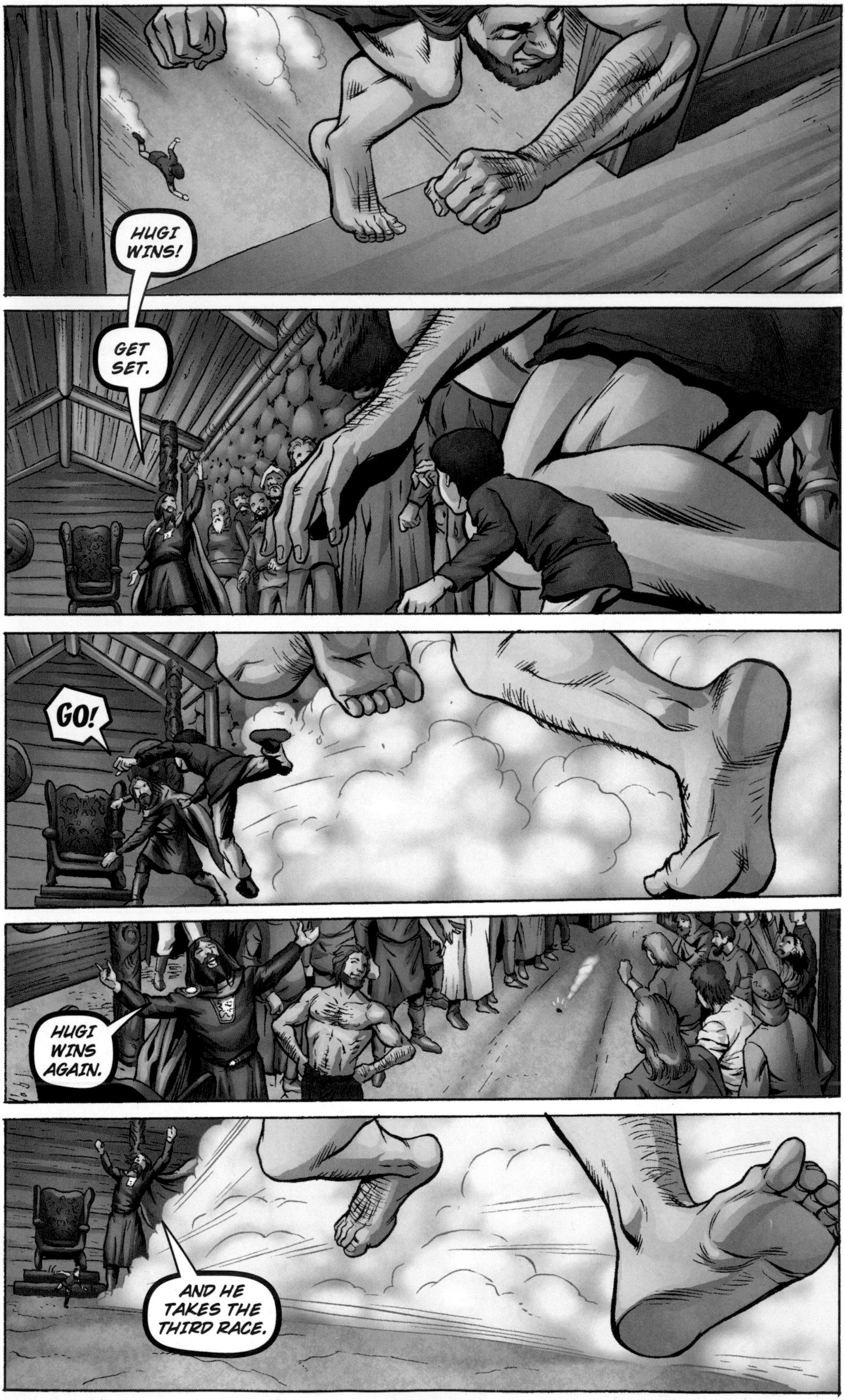
HUGI WINS!
GET SET.
GO!
HUGI WINS AGAIN.
AND HE TAKES THE THIRD RACE.

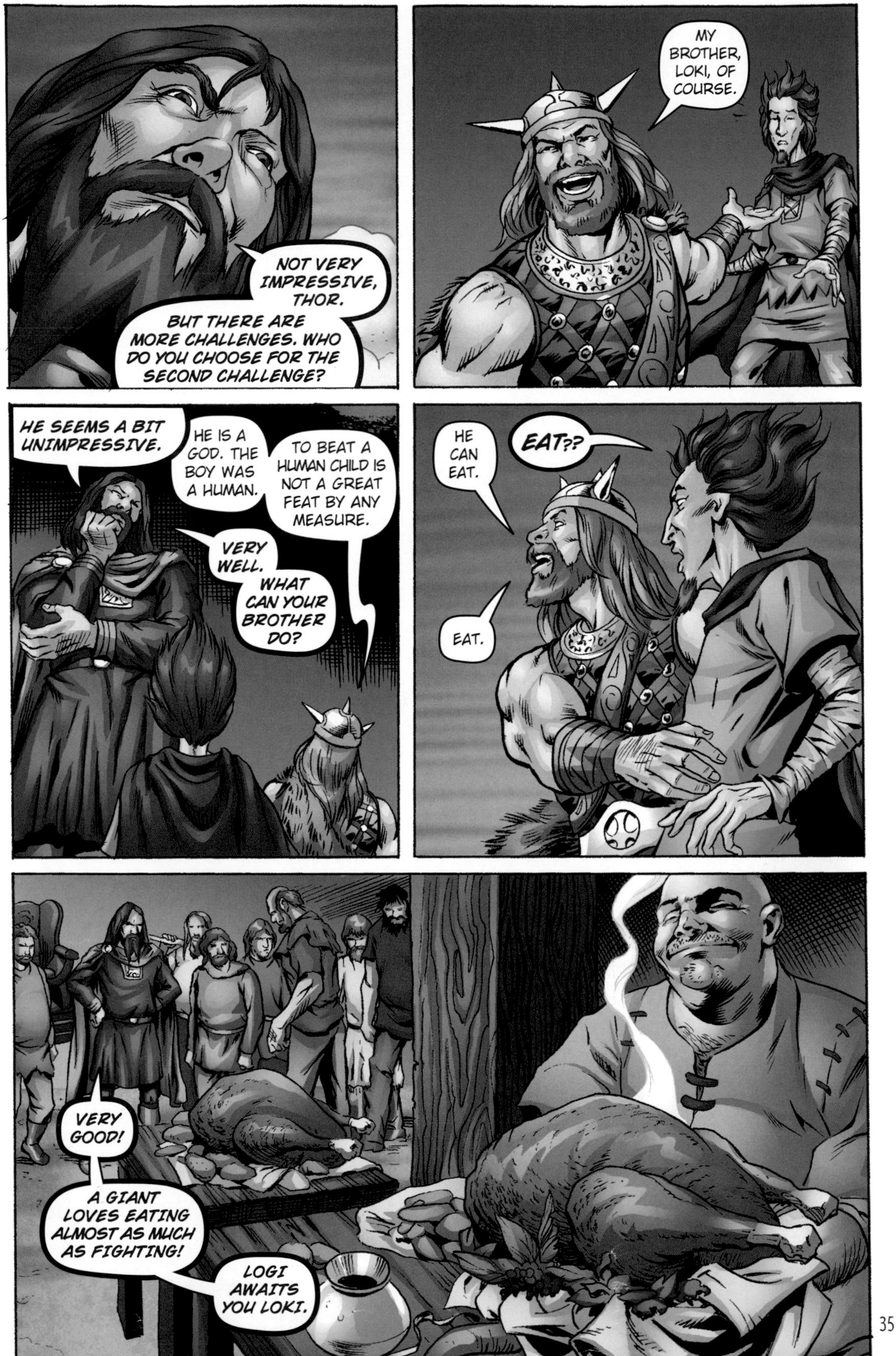
NOT VERY IMPRESSIVE, THOR.
BUT THERE ARE MORE CHALLENGES. WHO DO YOU CHOOSE FOR THE SECOND CHALLENGE?
MY BROTHER, LOKI, OF COURSE.
HE SEEMS A BIT UNIMPRESSIVE.
HE IS A GOD. THE BOY WAS A HUMAN.
TO BEAT A HUMAN CHILD IS NOT A GREAT FEAT BY ANY MEASURE.
VERY WELL.
WHAT CAN YOUR BROTHER DO?
HE CAN EAT.
EAT??
EAT.
VERY GOOD!
A GIANT LOVES EATING ALMOST AS MUCH AS FIGHTING!
LOGI AWAITS YOU LOKI.

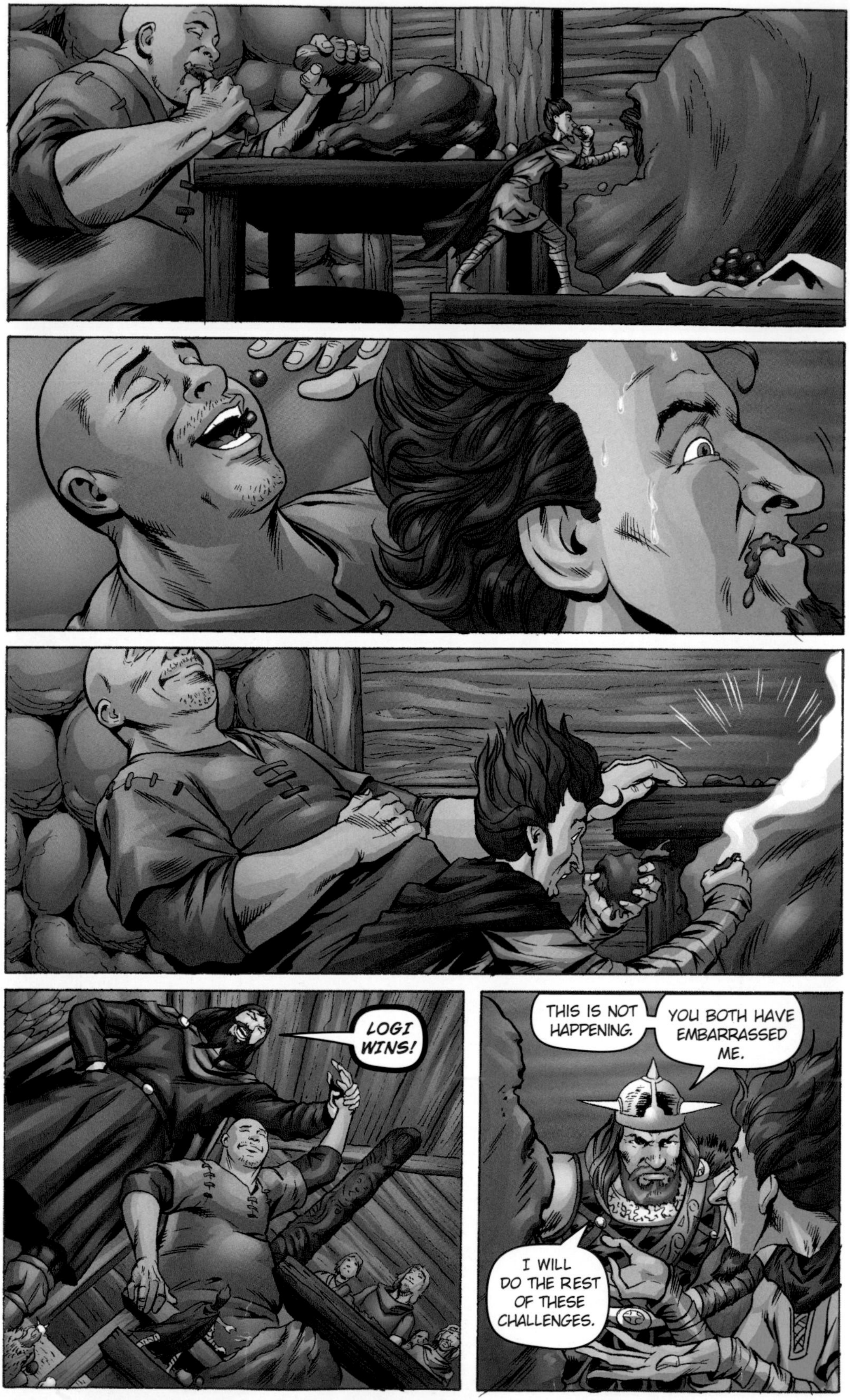
LOGI WINS!
THIS IS NOT HAPPENING.
YOU BOTH HAVE EMBARRASSED ME.
I WILL DO THE REST OF THESE CHALLENGES.

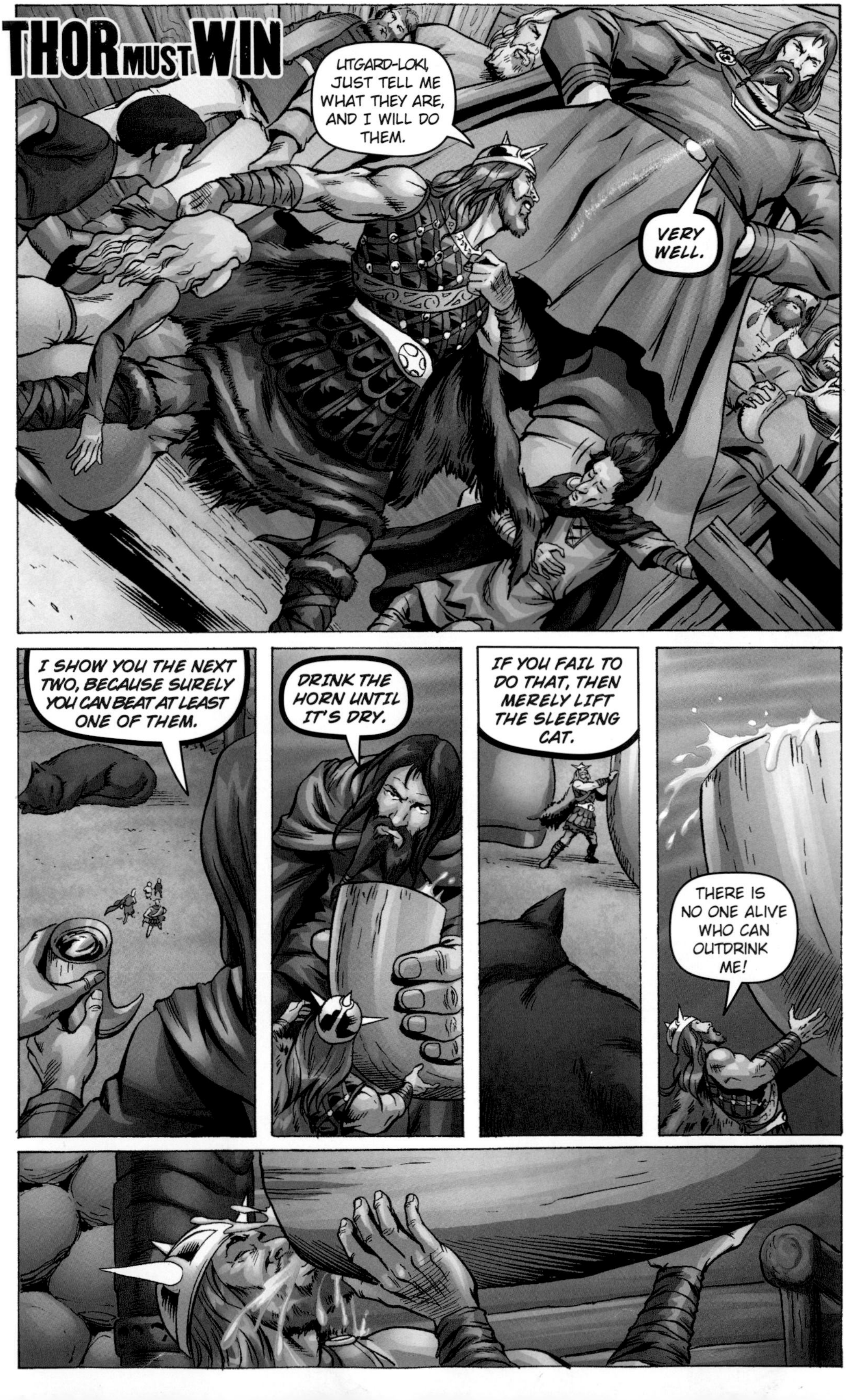
THOR MUST WIN
UTGARD-LOKI, JUST TELL ME WHAT THEY ARE, AND I WILL DO THEM.
VERY WELL.
I SHOW YOU THE NEXT TWO, BECAUSE SURELY YOU CAN BEAT AT LEAST ONE OF THEM.
DRINK THE HORN UNTIL IT'S DRY.
IF YOU FAIL TO DO THAT, THEN MERELY LIFT THE SLEEPING CAT.
THERE IS NO ONE ALIVE WHO CAN OUTDRINK ME!

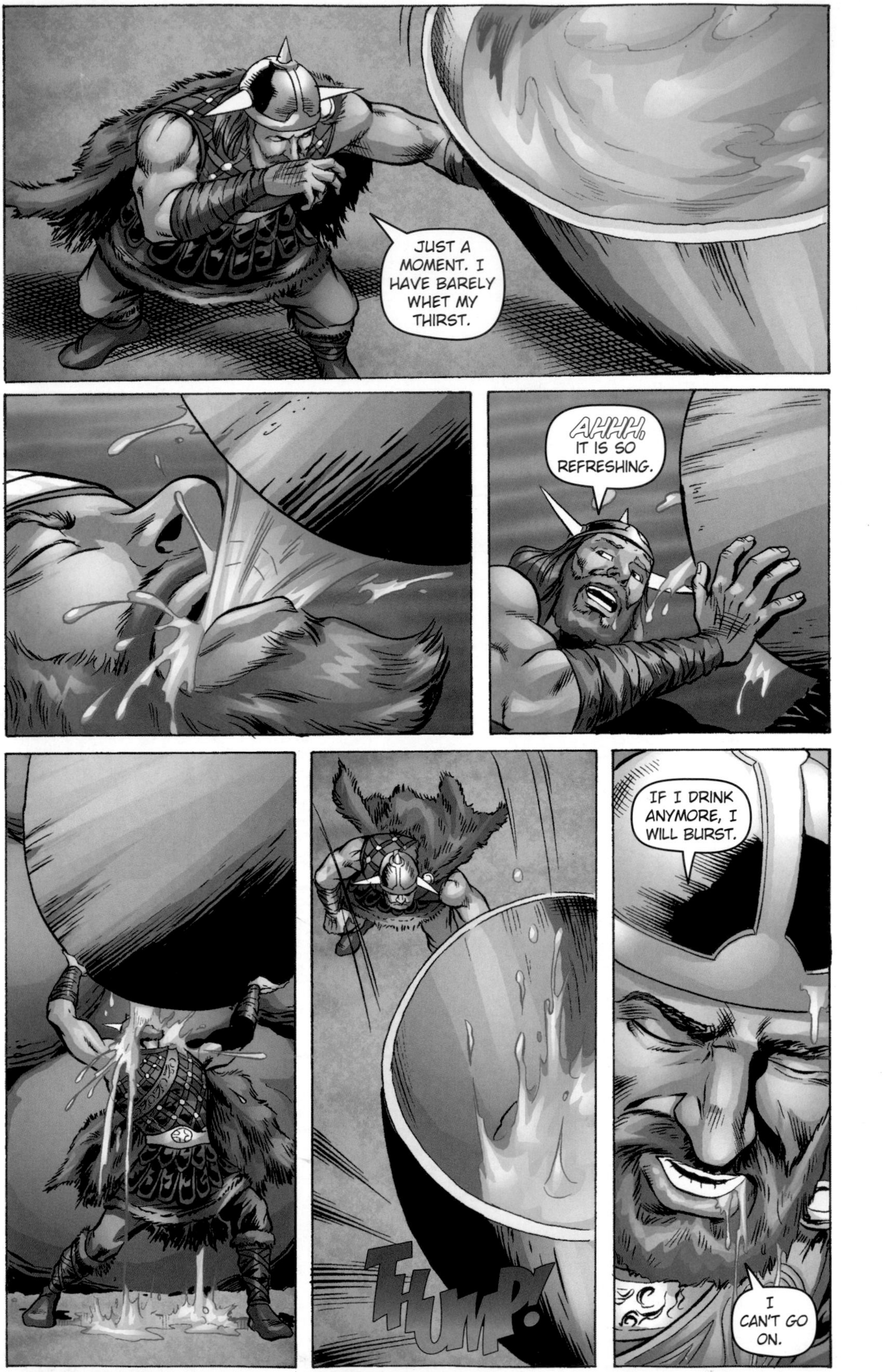
JUST A MOMENT. I HAVE BARELY WHET MY THIRST.
AHHH. IT IS SO REFRESHING.
THUMP!
IF I DRINK ANYMORE, I WILL BURST.
I CAN'T GO ON.

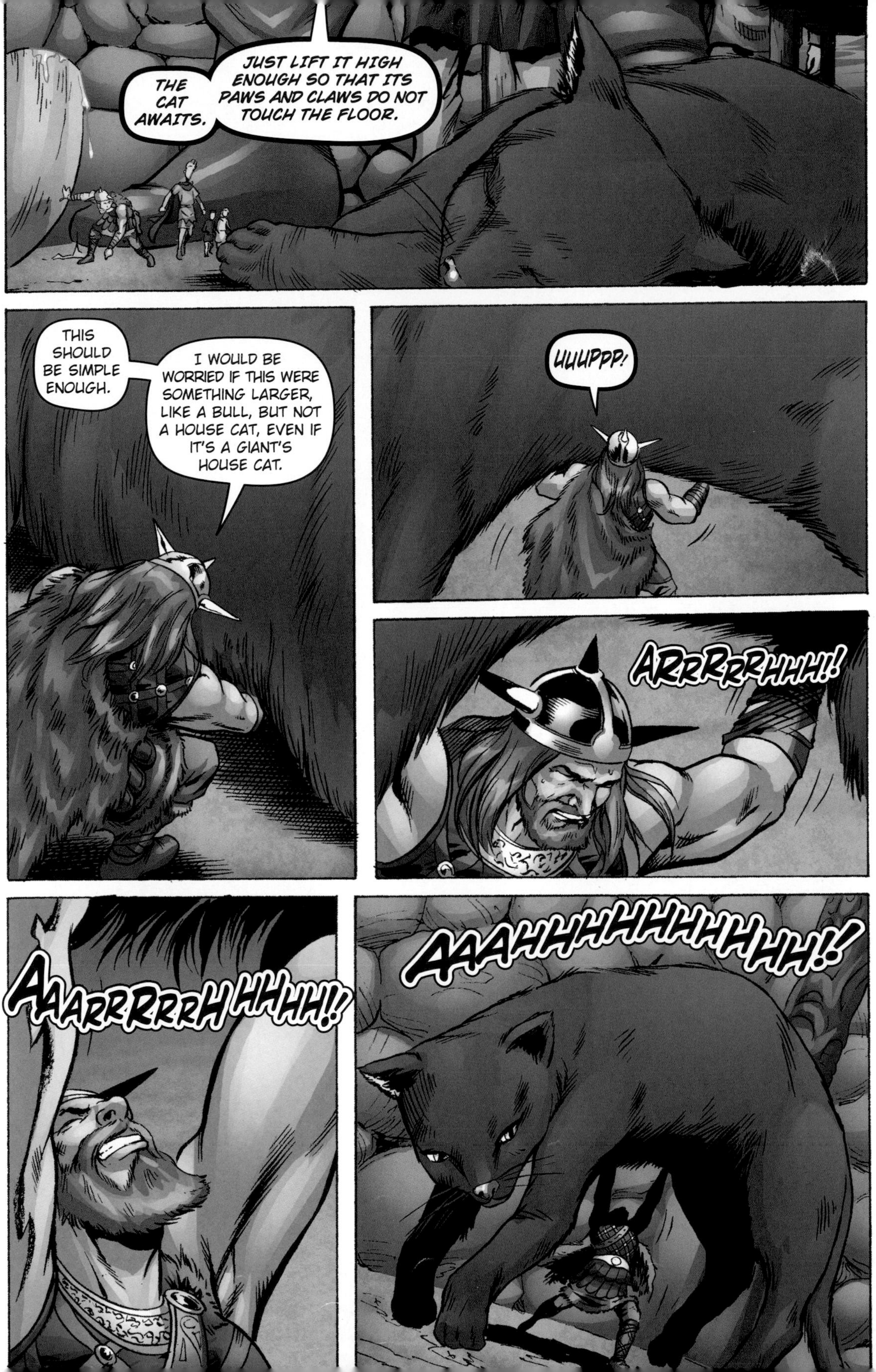
THE CAT AWAITS.
JUST LIFT IT HIGH ENOUGH SO THAT ITS PAWS AND CLAWS DO NOT TOUCH THE FLOOR.
THIS SHOULD BE SIMPLE ENOUGH.
I WOULD BE WORRIED IF THIS WERE SOMETHING LARGER, LIKE A BULL, BUT NOT A HOUSE CAT, EVEN IF IT'S A GIANT'S HOUSE CAT.
UUUPPP!
ARRRRRHHH!!
AAARRRRRRHHHHH!!
AAAHHHHHHHHHHHH!!

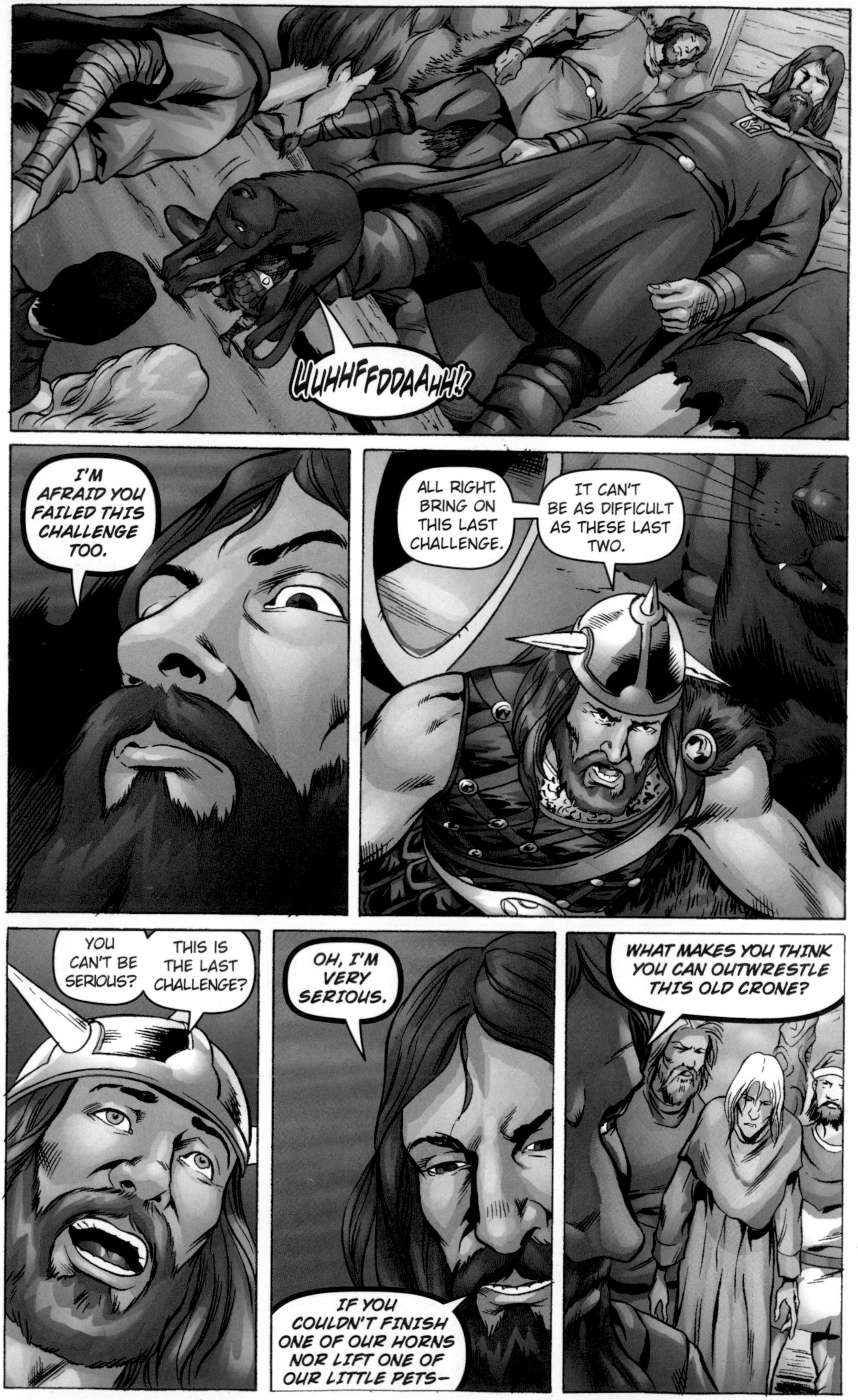
UUHHFFDDAAHH!!
I'M AFRAID YOU FAILED THIS CHALLENGE TOO.
ALL RIGHT. BRING ON THIS LAST CHALLENGE.
IT CAN'T BE AS DIFFICULT AS THESE LAST TWO.
YOU CAN'T BE SERIOUS?
THIS IS THE LAST CHALLENGE?
OH, I'M VERY SERIOUS.
IF YOU COULDN'T FINISH ONE OF OUR HORNS NOR LIFT ONE OF OUR LITTLE PETS-
WHAT MAKES YOU THINK YOU CAN OUTWRESTLE THIS OLD CRONE?

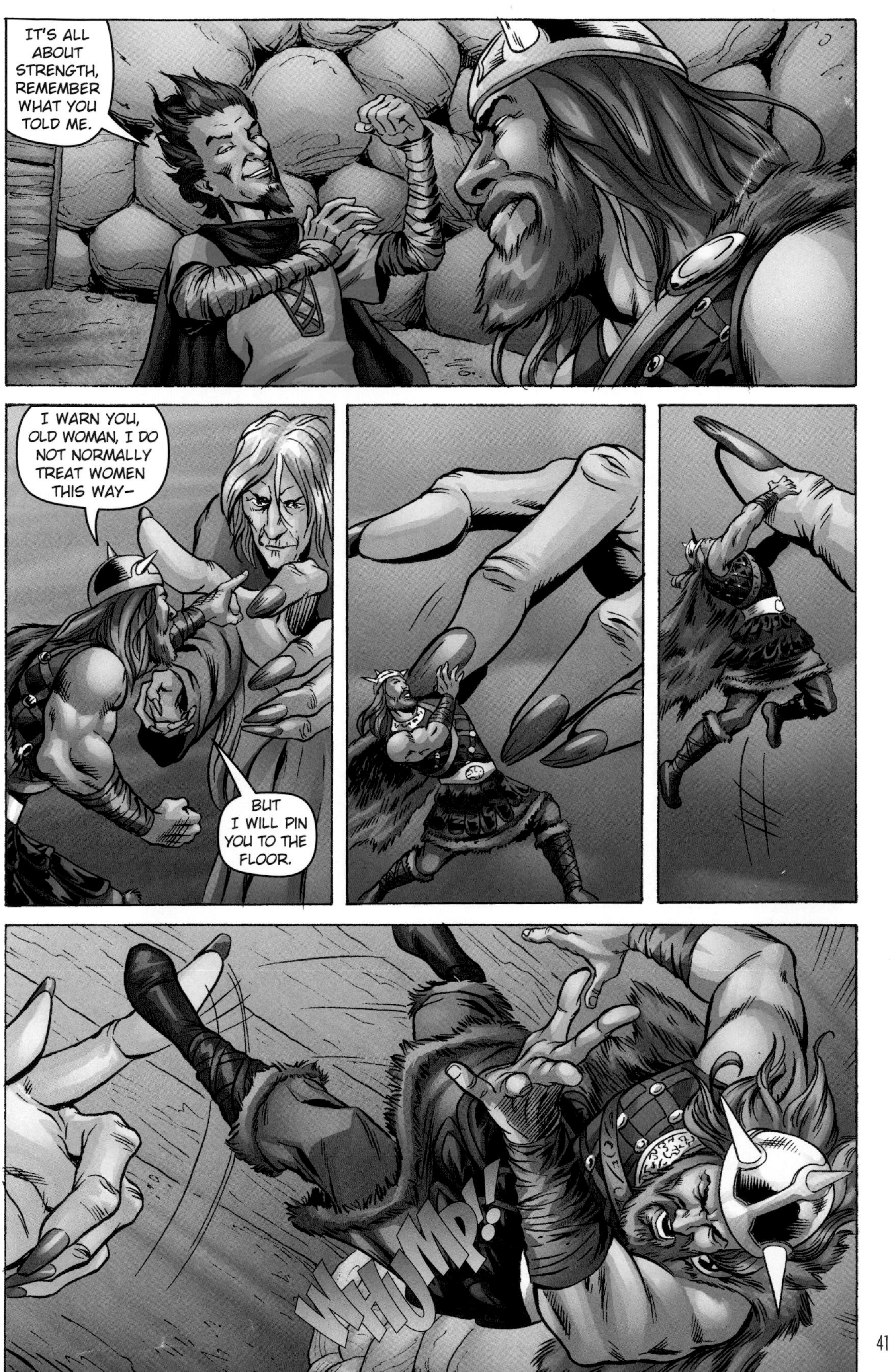
IT'S ALL ABOUT STRENGTH, REMEMBER WHAT YOU TOLD ME.
I WARN YOU, OLD WOMAN, I DO NOT NORMALLY TREAT WOMEN THIS WAY—
BUT I WILL PIN YOU TO THE FLOOR.
WHUMP!!

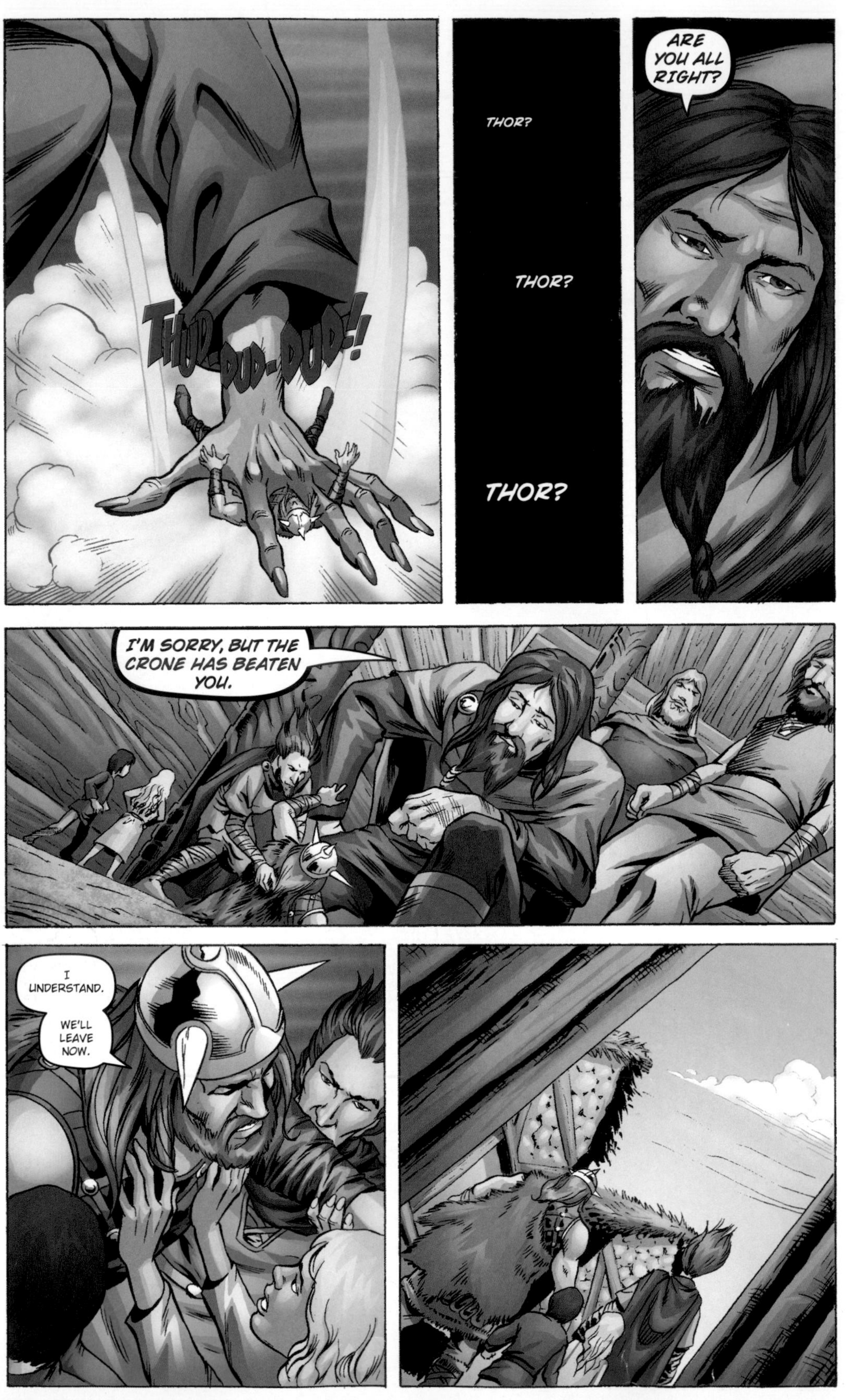
THUD-DUD-DUD!!
THOR?
THOR?
THOR?
ARE YOU ALL RIGHT?
I'M SORRY, BUT THE CRONE HAS BEATEN YOU.
I UNDERSTAND.
WE'LL LEAVE NOW.

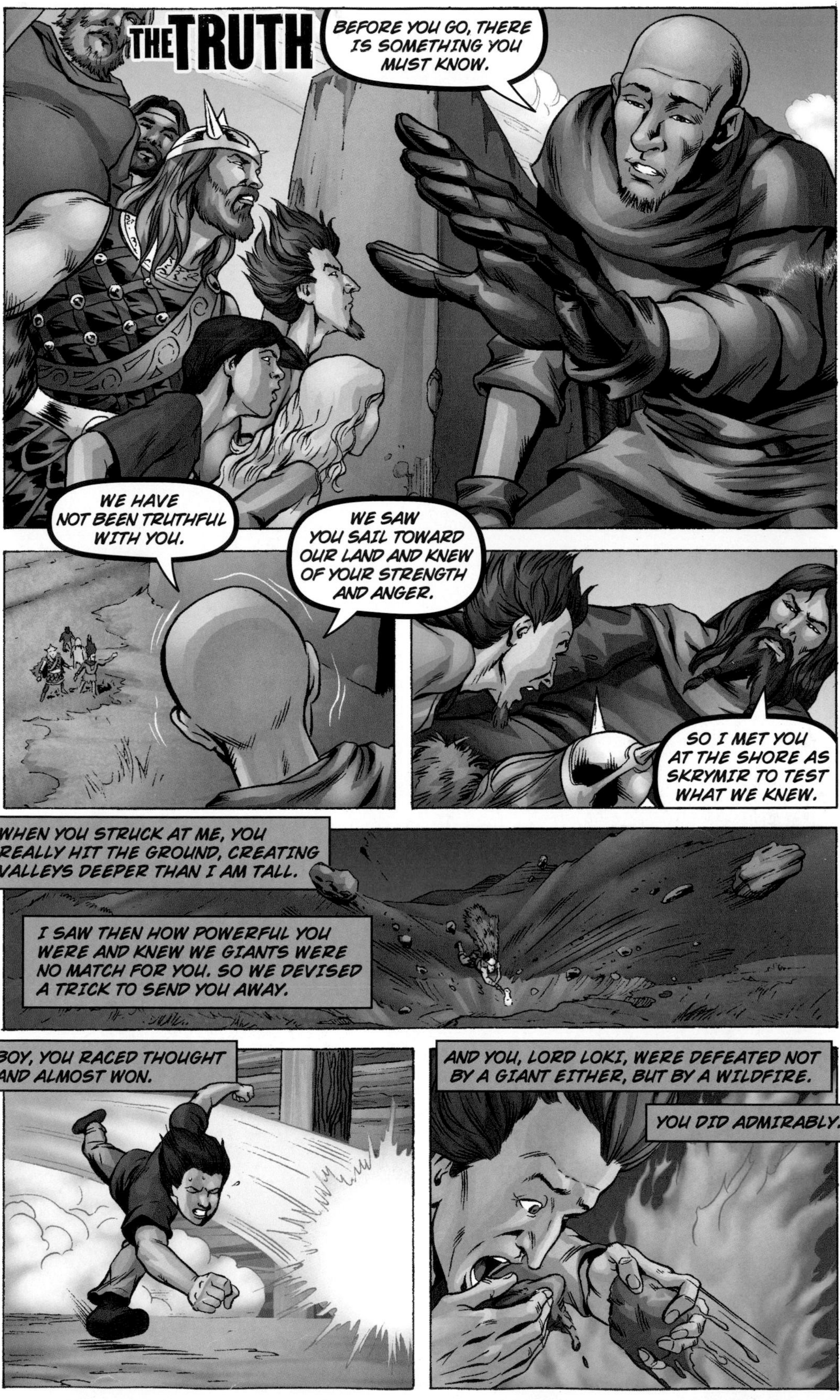
THE TRUTH
BEFORE YOU GO, THERE IS SOMETHING YOU MUST KNOW.
WE HAVE NOT BEEN TRUTHFUL WITH YOU.
WE SAW YOU SAIL TOWARD OUR LAND AND KNEW OF YOUR STRENGTH AND ANGER.
SO I MET YOU AT THE SHORE AS SKRYMIR TO TEST WHAT WE KNEW.
WHEN YOU STRUCK AT ME, YOU REALLY HIT THE GROUND, CREATING VALLEYS DEEPER THAN I AM TALL.
I SAW THEN HOW POWERFUL YOU WERE AND KNEW WE GIANTS WERE NO MATCH FOR YOU. SO WE DEVISED A TRICK TO SEND YOU AWAY.
BOY, YOU RACED THOUGHT AND ALMOST WON.
AND YOU, LORD LOKI, WERE DEFEATED NOT BY A GIANT EITHER, BUT BY A WILDFIRE.
YOU DID ADMIRABLY.

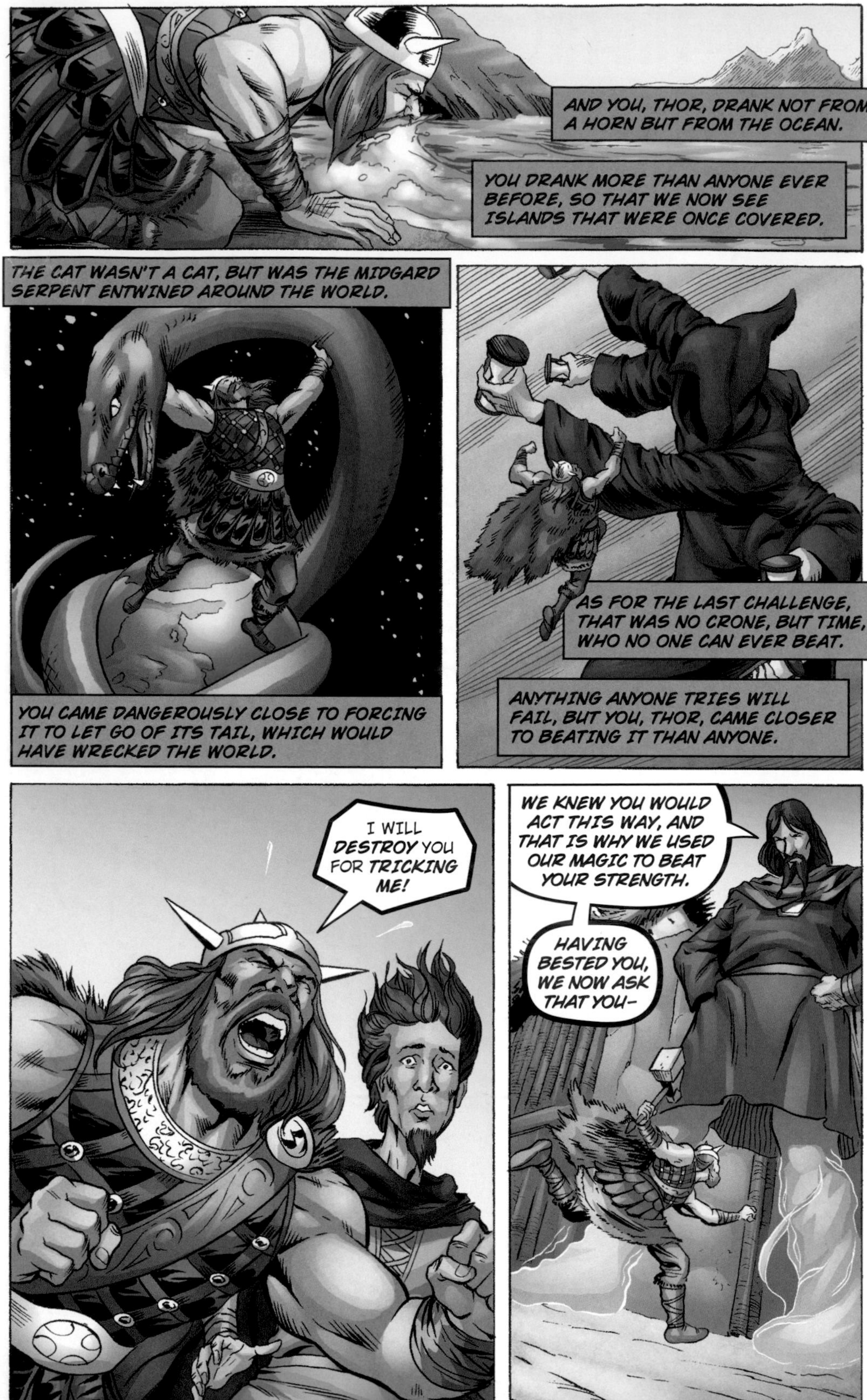
AND YOU, THOR, DRANK NOT FROM A HORN BUT FROM THE OCEAN.
YOU DRANK MORE THAN ANYONE EVER BEFORE, SO THAT WE NOW SEE ISLANDS THAT WERE ONCE COVERED.
THE CAT WASN'T A CAT, BUT WAS THE MIDGARD SERPENT ENTWINED AROUND THE WORLD.
YOU CAME DANGEROUSLY CLOSE TO FORCING IT TO LET GO OF ITS TAIL, WHICH WOULD HAVE WRECKED THE WORLD.
AS FOR THE LAST CHALLENGE, THAT WAS NO CRONE, BUT TIME, WHO NO ONE CAN EVER BEAT.
ANYTHING ANYONE TRIES WILL FAIL, BUT YOU, THOR, CAME CLOSER TO BEATING IT THAN ANYONE.
I WILL DESTROY YOU FOR TRICKING ME!
WE KNEW YOU WOULD ACT THIS WAY, AND THAT IS WHY WE USED OUR MAGIC TO BEAT YOUR STRENGTH.
HAVING BESTED YOU, WE NOW ASK THAT YOU-

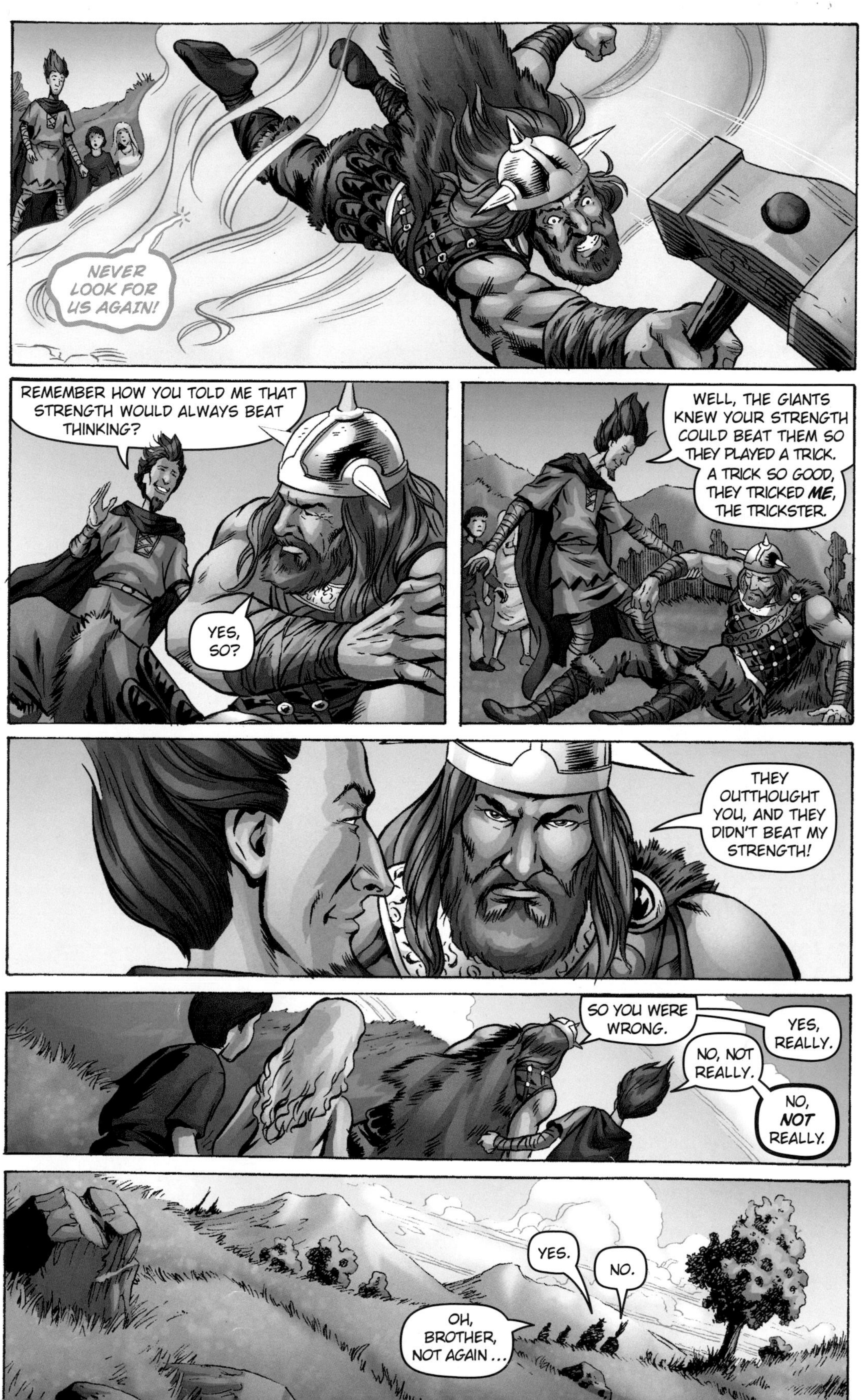
NEVER LOOK FOR US AGAIN!
REMEMBER HOW YOU TOLD ME THAT STRENGTH WOULD ALWAYS BEAT THINKING?
YES, SO?
WELL, THE GIANTS KNEW YOUR STRENGTH COULD BEAT THEM SO THEY PLAYED A TRICK. A TRICK SO GOOD, THEY TRICKED ***ME***, THE TRICKSTER.
THEY OUTTHOUGHT YOU, AND THEY DIDN'T BEAT MY STRENGTH!
SO YOU WERE WRONG.
NO, NOT REALLY.
YES, REALLY.
NO, ***NOT*** REALLY.
YES.
NO.
OH, BROTHER, NOT AGAIN . . .

GLOSSARY AND PRONUNCIATION GUIDE

ASGARD (*az*-gard): the home of the Norse gods

CRONE: an old woman

LEMMINGS: small, short-tailed, furry-footed rodents that live in northern regions

LOKI (*loh*-kee): the trickster in Norse mythology, often identified as Thor's brother

MIDGARD SERPENT: a giant serpent that circles the earth, according to Norse legend

MJOLNIR (my-uhl-*neer*): Thor's magic hammer

MORTAL: a being that dies

ODIN (*oh*-din): father of the Norse gods

THOR: the Norse god of Thunder

UTGARD-LOKI (*oot*-gard *loh*-kee): king of the Norse giants

pencil from page 32

FURTHER READING AND WEBSITES

Philip, Neil. *The Illustrated Book of Myths: Tales and Legends of the World.* New York: Dorling Kindersley, 1995. This illustrated book recounts myths from around the world, including Norse myths.

____. *Mythology.* New York: Dorling Kindersley, 1999. This volume in the Eyewitness Books series uses dozens of colorful photos and illustrations to explore myths from around the world.

Roberts, Morgan J. *Norse Gods and Heroes.* New York: Metro Books, 1995. Filled with illustrations and photos of ancient mythological artifacts, this book provides an excellent overview of Norse mythology.

Encyclopedia Mythica: Norse Mythology
http://www.pantheon.org/areas/mythology/europe/norse/articles.html
This helpful website features brief profiles of all of the Norse gods as well as information about many other characters in Norse mythology.

Thomas Bulfinch: Bulfinch's Mythology
http://www.classicreader.com/booktoc.php/sid.2/bookid.2823/
This website features one of the most popular English-language compilations of ancient myths. This classic work, which includes some Norse myths, was compiled by American Thomas Bulfinch in the 1800s.

CREATING *THOR AND LOKI: IN THE LAND OF GIANTS*

To create the story of Thor and Loki's journey to the land of giants, author Jeff Limke relied heavily on the classic book *Bulfinch's Mythology* by American Thomas Bulfinch. This work drew its material from the *Prose Edda*, a compilation of Norse tales compiled by Icelandic poet and lawyer Snorri Sturluson. Artist Ron Randall consulted numerous reference books on the medieval Vikings as well as art from the ancient Norse period to bring to life the vivid images of this story.

INDEX

ABOUT THE AUTHOR AND THE ARTIST

JEFF LIMKE was raised in North Dakota. There he read, listened to, and marveled at stories from the day he learned to read. He later taught stories for many years, and he has written adaptations of them. Some of his stories have been published by Caliber Comics, Arrow Comics, and Kenzer and Company. Along the way he got married, and he and his wife had a daughter who loves to read, listen to, and marvel at stories.

RON RANDALL has drawn comics for every major comic publisher in the United States, including Marvel, DC, Image and Dark Horse. He has worked on super hero comics such as *Justice League* and *Spiderman*, science fiction titles such as *Star Wars*, *Star Trek* and his own creation *Trekker*, fantasy adventure titles such as *DragonLance* and *Warlord*, and suspense and horror titles including *SwampThing*, *Predator*, and *Venom*. He lives in Portland, Oregon.